Monastic Ecological Wisdom

A Living Tradition

Samuel Torvend

LITURGICAL PRESS

Collegeville, Minnesota

www.litpress.org

Cover art: Cistercian monks at work. Alexander of Bremen. Expositio en Apocalypsim (University Library Cambridge Ms. Mm 5.31 fol. 113).

1   2   3   4   5   6   7   8   9

Library of Congress Cataloging-in-Publication Data.

Names: Torvend, Samuel, author.
Title: Monastic ecological wisdom : a living tradition / Samuel Torvend.
Description: Collegeville, Minnesota : Liturgical Press, [2023] |
    Includes bibliographical references and index. | Summary:
    "Inspired by Pope Francis's encyclical, Laudato Sí, and Benedictine
    communities around the world whose shared monastic values
    inform ecological practice, Monastic Ecological Wisdom explores
    how early medieval monasteries serve as a model of sustainable
    development and environmental conservation in today's world"—
    Provided by publisher.
Identifiers: LCCN 2023017429 (print) | LCCN 2023017430 (ebook) |
    ISBN 9780814667972 (paperback) | ISBN 9780814667989 (epub) |
    ISBN 9798400800559 (pdf)
Subjects: LCSH: Human ecology—Religious aspects—Christianity. |
    Environmental ethics. | Monastic and religious life.
Classification: LCC BT695.5 .T68 2023 (print) | LCC BT695.5 (ebook) |
    DDC 261.8/8—dc23/eng/20230829
LC record available at https://lccn.loc.gov/2023017429
LC ebook record available at https://lccn.loc.gov/2023017430

In loving memory of

SUSAN PALO CHERWIEN
1953–2021

Distinguished hymnwriter

Friend of the earth

Companion to many

"In his impressively researched *Monastic Ecological Wisdom*, Samuel Torvend sifts through scholarly literature on environmental history, church history, and biographies/hagiographies of Benedict of Nursia in order to demonstrate the values that are timely in our current ecological distress—values such as attention to local ecology, friendship with other creatures, humility, and simplicity—are in fact hallmarks of Benedictine spirituality. Readers will come away from this book with renewed appreciation for the deep resonances between Christian discipleship and responsible care for the Earth. *Monastic Ecological Wisdom* is well suited for use in classrooms, parish discussion groups, and individual reading."

> — Timothy Brunk, associate professor of theology, Villanova University

"This is a book of insights and connections, many of which may surprise you. Torvend reveals parallels between the destructive patterns of the Roman Empire in the time of Jesus and our contemporary ecological and social crises. He proposes St. Benedict's monastic approach to life and the natural world as an antidote to the sins of the past and the present: a wisdom that sought a pattern of interaction with the environment that was sustainable for centuries, respecting the land and all creatures as God's creation and God's possession. The Gospels proclaimed a revolutionary message against the idolatry and rapaciousness of the Roman Empire, a message that still challenges similar forces today. We need an alternative way of life to confront our sins against creation. Benedict and Torvend show us the way."

> — Lawrence E. Mick, a priest of the Archdiocese of Cincinnati and author of *Liturgy and Ecology in Dialogue*

"*Monastic Ecological Wisdom* tells us the inspiring story of how the life of St. Benedict influenced the way he would see God's creation as a way of encounter with the divine. Samuel Torvend speaks to the present historical situation in a way that sees the riches of St. Benedict's 1,500-year-old Rule as relevant to our present situation. The connections between St. Benedict's Rule and *Laudato Si'*, as presented here, inspire a careful reading of both these early and contemporary documents."

> — Abbot Primate Gregory Polan, OSB, Badia Sant'Anselmo, Rome, Italy

"It can be tempting to think that current experiences of climatic change, environmental degradation, and institutional corruption are so unique that we have nothing to learn from the past. But such thinking is impossible after you read Samuel Torvend's *Monastic Ecological Wisdom* and immerse yourself into the deep and sustainable wisdom of ancient and medieval Christian communities. This important book richly explores environmental practices and structures of Benedictine life, the roots of those practices in the Christian tradition, and the possibilities for contemporary Christian faith based in justice and the land."

> — Kevin J. O'Brien, author of *The Violence of Climate Change*

"The book is a thoughtful effort to respond to the challenge and insight of *Laudato Si'* with the riches of the Benedictine tradition and the spirituality of the Rule of Benedict. It is a work that will surely encourage many, including me, to harvest its insights and to continue to respond to the needs of the poor and the environment."

> — Right Reverend John Klassen, OSB, abbot of Saint John's Abbey

Contents

Introduction   ix

Chapter 1
Early Christian Resistance to Imperial Domination of the Earth   1

Chapter 2
Benedict's Journey Out of Imperial Christianity   28

Chapter 3
Benedict's Refuge in Nature   53

Chapter 4
Praying the Seasons of Life on God's Earth   75

Chapter 5
An Environmental Rule   97

Chapter 6
Monastic Ecological Values   117

Chapter 7
The Land Is in the Church   139

Bibliography   145

Index   156

Introduction

Who could have known that a poor friar from a medieval hill town would inspire a pope of the twenty-first century to publish an encyclical that has animated Catholics, other Christians, environmentalists, and scientists throughout the world? With the 2015 publication of *Laudato Si'* (On Care for Our Common Home), Pope Francis presented a pathway toward the future of environmental conservation and the healing of a wound inflicted on the earth since the onset of the Industrial Revolution. And yet, his insightful assessment of human responsibility for earth's suffering included what many have claimed is a quietly subversive denunciation of how wealthy nations tend to view the poorer peoples of the earth: as nothing more than expendable laborers who serve at the whim of those committed to unsustainable economic growth. In *Laudato Si'*, Pope Francis holds the two together; care for a wounded earth is inextricably linked with care for its most vulnerable people. Once published, the encyclical prompted Catholics, the Eastern Orthodox, Anglicans, and Protestants to praise its insightful analysis of global warming and its proposals for renewing the planet and its people affected by pollution, chemical poisoning, and climate change. He thus shed light on care for the earth and its many creatures as a *spiritual practice* in the largest Christian communion on the face of the planet.

In the following year, the Permanent Delegation of Italy to the United Nations Educational, Scientific, and Cultural Organization (UNESCO) made a public application, requesting that UNESCO designate eight early medieval monastic complexes as World Heritage Sites, thus ensuring their protection in perpetuity. These included the Monasteries of San Benedetto and Santa Scolastica at Subiaco and the monastic complex at Monte Cassino. Justification for the designation of these monastic complexes included not only their architectural and artistic merit but also the ways in which they "fit harmoniously into the natural environment . . . and offer a model of coexistence, sustainable development, and conservation of the environment, providing a valuable message for contemporary society and for future generations."[1] Such a claim raises the question: How is it that early medieval monasteries might serve today as a model of sustainable development and environmental conservation in a time of rapid urban development and global warming?

I live in the Pacific Northwest, where the effects of global warming have been experienced with greater frequency in the last ten years. With unusually warm temperatures, widespread and volatile forest fires produce toxic smoke so strong that venturing outdoors is viewed as dangerous to the health of humans and other creatures. The growth of volatile storms, combined with unchecked deforestation, produces life-threatening flooding with destruction of homes, churches, schools, and businesses—destruction unknown to previous generations. Superfund sites mar the beauty of the Puget Sound region and make one think twice before consuming fish or shellfish found close to these sites poisoned by human folly. Unchecked urban development is diminishing the tree canopy in a region that had been known for its evergreen and oxygen-producing forests. The harm to soil, water, forest, animals, and humans is no abstraction; it is not something happening only in another part of the world. It is in our backyard. Is it a far-fetched notion to imagine that monastic values and practices

---

[1] Permanent Delegation of Italy to UNESCO, "The Cultural Landscape of the Benedictine Settlements in Medieval Italy," March 18, 2016, accessed on July 16, 2022, at https://whc.unesco.org/en/tentativelists/6107/.

could assist in the careful conservation of what we claim is God's first gift, God's first gesture of grace: the earth and all that dwells within it?

This study of monastic ecological wisdom is inspired by the publication of *Laudato Si'*; the designation of early medieval monastic communities as centers of environmental conservation; the heroic work of social ethicists, theologians, scientists, and environmental activists; and resistance to the false notion that the primary ideological culprit in the degradation of the earth and its many diverse creatures is Christianity. While there are, in fact, a good number of Christian leaders and communities who couldn't care less about the fate of the earth,[2] they do not represent the majority of Christians—among whom are Catholics, the largest number of Christians in the world. This study finds inspiration in the monastic communities of the world where we find thoughtful stewardship of land, water sources, forests, orchards, wetlands, buildings, and diverse creatures—communities whose shared monastic values inform ecological practice. I mention here Saint John's Abbey in Collegeville, Minnesota, and the Monastery of Christ in the Desert outside of Abiquiu, New Mexico—two communities in which care for the local ecology is prominent.

One might say that this study holds together two fields: environmental history and church history. Given the latter, the first chapter considers recent New Testament research that suggests early Christians (from whom monastic communities arose) were aware of the ecological dimensions of their faith, reflected both in liturgical practice and in texts that claimed that the God known in Jesus Christ—*not* the Roman emperor (or any political leader, for that matter)—is the author of all life on earth. Thus, the first chapter sets forth the earth-awareness

---

[2] Let us keep in mind that there are a good many other spiritual traditions, ideologies, political leaders, governments, and multinational corporations that view the earth as nothing more than an object to use and then throw away.

among early Christians, an awareness that has often been overlooked in both church and environmental histories. The second chapter presents an overview of early Christian practice prior to the imperialization of the church in 380 by Emperor Theodosius. This is the context in which we consider Benedict of Nursia: a young man who became disillusioned with not only his privileged classmates and studies but also the conflicts and contradictions of a church that was influenced (if not seriously shaped) by Roman imperial values and practices.

Chapter 3 relies in part on the work of paleoecologists in their reconstruction of the natural habitat in which Benedict lived while in Subiaco. Here we suggest that the young hermit and soon-to-be reformer was well acquainted with the land, water sources, vegetation, and animals of the Subiacan ravine where he lived for three years. A "sense of place" first seen in Subiaco would soon inform Benedict's insistence on "stability of place" in the Rule of Benedict. We consider how the "nature miracles" recorded by Pope Gregory I in his hagiography of Benedict reveal the natural topography with which Benedict interacted. At the same time, Benedict is one of many early monastics who encouraged friendship with birds, fish, and animals—thus the significance of the raven.

Chapter 4 leads into the practice of prayer (*ora*) and argues for an ecological interpretation of communal prayer throughout the day and the natural seasons of the year as described by Benedict in the Rule. Scholarly consensus suggests that Benedict relied on but revised the Rule of the Master and was also influenced by other existing rules, such as the one composed by St. Basil. What we find with Benedict will come as no surprise to many readers: he is flexible in offering future generations a certain latitude in structuring daily prayer while establishing a pattern of daily and seasonal prayer tied to solar and lunar rhythms and the changing seasons of the year. Here we highlight what may often be overlooked today: that the Christian practice of common prayer and the keeping of the liturgical seasons and feasts are inextricably linked to the movements of the heavens and the earth—not to the market or the work schedule.

In chapter 5, we consider the *labora* that flows from *ora*. Here we rely in part on the work of Benedictine scholars who have commented on the ecological significance of select chapters in the Rule: Terrence Kardong, OSB; John Klassen, OSB; Philip Lawrence, OSB; and Judith Sutera, OSB. Of course, this is not to suggest that in his description of prayer and labor Benedict intended to compose a treatise on environmental ethics. Rather, it is to claim that an ecophilic lens can help us recognize ecological values and practices in the Rule that may have been overlooked by previous generations who believed the primary goal of Christian and monastic life was entrance into everlasting life, an afterlife enjoyed elsewhere. Here we highlight the labor and careful stewardship of land and water sources by early medieval monastic communities—a labor frequently overlooked in environmental histories.

Chapter 6 invites the reader to consider the contemporary relevance of monastic ecological wisdom as witnessed in its values and practices and how they might inform sustainable stewardship of one's local habitat, one's natural ecology, today. One should not assume that this chapter or this book serves as a strategy to diminish or end global warming or other forms of earth's degradation. Rather, it is an invitation to recognize that from the ritual center of Christian faith and life—the Mass—and from a sacramental imagination that recognizes the presence of God everywhere, there arises an *acclamation*, "The earth is the Lord's and all that is in it,"[3] and a *conviction*, "All things came into being through [the Word], and without him not one thing came into being."[4] At the heart of Christian

---

[3] Psalm 24:1.
[4] John 1:3.

faith and life is Jesus Christ, "the firstborn of all creation,"[5] the One who continues to invite his followers to conserve and protect his earth as careful stewards rather than wasteful owners.

Chapter 7 describes how a geologist discerned the presence of the local land in a monastic church and how that chance encounter drew him into the practice of faith. Here we consider how awareness of one's local place—its land, water, animals, and trees—can lead to recognition of those who suffer the effects of environmental degradation and the promise of a new earth.

In this study, I speak of Benedict as a reformer who gave birth to a reform movement. This is not to say that he holds no other significance in the life of the church, to the many communities who follow his Rule, among students and scholars of early medieval history, and among the growing number of his oblates throughout the world. Yes, he is a searcher for God, a tutor in prayer, a wise legislator, a compassionate abbot, and an exemplar of holiness. And yet, as with all people, he cannot be reduced to one meaning, one significance. There flows from him a surplus of meaning. To suggest that he was and remains a reformer is to recognize the more public and social dimension of his life, his Rule, and his spiritual progeny. It is to suggest what the pioneering monk, Virgil Michel, OSB, knew so well: "Too long have sincere Christians looked upon their spiritual life as something shut up entirely within themselves and have tried to harden themselves against the world even while leaving the world to itself. We must be with Christ . . .; we must . . . affect the world in which we live."[6] Here we suggest that Benedict's reforming project held

---

[5] Colossians 1:15.

[6] From Michel's unpublished manuscript, "Liturgy and Catholic Life," as quoted in Paul Marx, OSB, *Virgil Michel and the Liturgical Movement* (Collegeville, MN: Liturgical Press, 1957), 262.

within it a certain ecological wisdom revealed in the values and practices of his followers, a wisdom that can still "affect the world in which we live."

To these friends and colleagues, I offer my thanks: Amelia Carroll; David Cherwien; Jennifer Forman; John Forman, OblSB; Charles Searls-Ridge, OblSB; Benjamin Stewart and my colleagues in the Ecology and Liturgy Seminar of the North American Academy of Liturgy; the staff of Alcuin Library at Saint John's University; Isidore Glyer, OSB; Ephrem Hollermann, OSB; Michael Peterson, OSB; Joseph Schneeweis, OSB; and the oblates of Saint John's Abbey. Funding for research in central Italy was made possible, in part, by a Phillips Regency Award, a Benson-Starkovich Award, and a diocesan travel grant. I offer my thanks to Luigi Lanzi, who made possible visits to the archeological remains of San Vincenzo al Volturno and to the Monasteries of San Benedetto and Santa Scolastica in Subiaco. I am grateful for the support I received from Melisa Anderson, Joanna Gregson, Erik Hammerstrom, Jen Hasson, and Kevin O'Brien. I give thanks for my father, E. Silas Torvend (+), and my mother, Alice Kjesbu Torvend (+), who throughout their lives steadfastly cared for the earth and its many creatures. I also give thanks for Sean Horner, Rebecca Torvend, and Rex Torvend Rainsberger, whose love knows no bounds. I offer my thanks to Timothy Brunk for his keen editorial eye. I offer my thanks to Hans Christoffersen of Liturgical Press for his remarkable patience, keen insight, and support, and to Monica Bokinskie, Tara Durheim, Stephanie Lancour, Jamie Lauer, and Michelle Verkuilen, who have brought the book to life.

Ut In Omnibus, Glorificetur Deus.
December 28, 2022
Feast of the Holy Innocents, Martyrs

1

Early Christian Resistance to Imperial Domination of the Earth

As a young student, I was taught that the Roman Empire was the greatest empire on the face of the earth. My teachers invited me to marvel at its military expertise, its far-flung and impressive road system that supported rapid troop movements, its monumental buildings intended to evoke awe and the feeling of "littleness" in the viewer, its reverence for law and legal codes, and its economic dominance over many tribes and nations through a highly ordered program of colonial control. Indeed, the power and legacy of imperial Rome did not die with its gradual demise but rather inspired the creation of the Holy Roman Empire, the creation of the British Empire, Mussolini's dream of ruling East Africa and Western Asia, Hitler's Third Reich, and the oft-repeated claim by government leaders of every political persuasion that "America is the greatest nation on the face of the earth." Over the past fifty years, however, historians have highlighted another dimension of the Roman Empire, one that brings into stark relief the life and work of Jesus, his first companions, and the early Christian communities that gathered around a table for the breaking of the bread, what came to be known as the Mass.

The evangelist Luke alludes to this Roman context when, in the second chapter of his gospel, he mentions Emperor Augustus, the Roman governor of Syria who supervised Roman Palestine, and the small towns of Nazareth and Bethlehem (which would have been under Roman control). Throughout his short public life, Jesus proclaimed the advent of the kingdom of God in both word and action. That he used a political term—*kingdom*—and a theological term—*God*—would have raised troubling questions, if not criticism, among those who knew of only one kingdom: that of the emperor. At the end of Jesus' life, the evangelists invoke the military presence of Rome with the mention of Pontius Pilate, the torture of Jesus by Roman guards, and his execution by crucifixion—a form of capital punishment widely used by Rome to suppress any resistance to its authority. Not long after Jesus' death, Christians began to pray at the site of Peter's execution next to the Mons Vaticanus in Rome, and Luke reports that Paul preached in the capital, the heart of this vast empire. Rome is ever present throughout the life of Jesus and the first Christians, yet present, it would seem, through brief mention and allusion.

The Savior of the World

What we know of the kingdom of Caesar Augustus is this: it was a colonizing power that used deadly military force to conquer new land and peoples for economic gain and to suppress any and every form of opposition to its oppressive presence. It was a society that valued patriarchy and placed all legal and social power in males, a society that sanctioned the legal ownership of women by men and the legal right of every father to smother his newborn infant if he did not want the child. It was a society that had little regard for the virtue of mercy, a quality of relationship it viewed as pathological, as something to be avoided by all free males who valued their public reputations. Indeed, massive poverty and a slave economy were supported by the conviction that mercy and compassion should never be shown to those who suffer—for the gods had decreed their sad status in life, and who would ever provoke the anger of the gods by questioning their judgment? And it was a society that flocked to the arena, the Colosseum, for its most popular form of entertainment: the maiming, torturing, and killing of gladiators, colonized slaves, animals, and, in time, the followers of Jesus Christ.

We also know that imperial Romans and their colonized peoples were expected to give their loyalty, their worship, to the Roman emperor and the gods of the state, in particular Mars, the god of war, who through rape became the progenitor of the murderous twins Romulus and Remus. While Luke notes that angels sang "Glory to God in the highest heaven" and announced the birth of a Savior and Lord on earth,[1] every person in the empire would have known that *before* the birth of Jesus, only the emperor held such exalted titles. After all, his full appellation, one that mixed both politics and religion, was *Imperator Caesar Divi Filius Augustus*: "Commander (One Who Alone Rules), From the House of Julius Caesar, Son of the Divine One, Sacred Majesty." "We set up altars to swear by your name, Augustus," wrote the Roman lyric poet Horace, "and we acknowledge that nothing like you has come into existence before your birth or will exist after your death."[2] In his poem on the Roman calendar, the imperial poet Ovid transformed the emperor Augustus into the highest god when he wrote, "You have long been Father of the World. On earth you have the name of Jupiter who reigns in the highest heaven."[3] "You shall call me your Lord and your God," demanded one emperor.[4] "O Savior of the World," exclaimed

---

[1] Luke 2:14.
[2] Horace, *Epistles* 2.1.15.
[3] Ovid, *Fasti* 2.127, 130–31.
[4] Suetonius, *Vita Domitiani* 13.

Propertius, the poet from Assisi, "the land—all the land—is yours!"[5] A clearer statement of imperial control over every inch of soil and every watery body under Rome's dominion could not have been made. The land, water sources, flora and fauna, fields, forests, minerals, and vineyards of Rome and its many territories constituted the *patria* of the *pater*, the expansive "homeland" of the "father"—the son of God, the savior, the lord of lords: the emperor. Without batting an eye, Roman poets created panegyrics—imperial propaganda—in praise of the emperor who ruled over and thus controlled the earth and its rich treasures.

Let it be said that under the Republic the Romans admired the natural world and recognized their dependence on its fertility. It was considered a sacred place in which the gods of nature ruled: Terra Mater, the earth goddess; Neptune, god of the sea; Volturnus, god of all rivers; Diana, the divine protector of animals; Ceres, goddess of grain and agriculture; Bacchus, god of the vineyard and wine; and Silvanus, god of the forests. "For the ancients," writes J. Donald Hughes, "the natural environment was endowed with living, divine beings who maintained its order and resisted the ill-considered actions of human beings. Because of their presence, the ancients felt that acts of social injustice could bring environmental punishments and that the gods could manifest their wrath in natural disasters."[6]

One wonders: Did the emergence of the emperor as the lord and master of the earth displace the earlier worship of earth's gods, who were thought to resist human acts against the natural world? Or was it the work of philosophers who diminished the role of the gods as they sought a more pragmatic understanding of the natural world? Did their rejection of

---

[5] Sextus Propertius, *Elegies* 4.6.

[6] J. Donald Hughes, *Environmental Problems of the Greeks and Romans: Ecology in the Ancient Mediterranean* (Baltimore: Johns Hopkins University Press, 2014), 51.

Roman mythology and their search for a "scientific" appreciation of the environment inadvertently participate in the objectification of lands and seas, vegetative and animal life—an
objectification that robbed the natural world of its soul and
made it easier to use and even abuse? And, then, what of those
worldviews that considered matter itself to be base, if not evil,
a prison for the rational mind or soul? If, as the Neoplatonists
taught, the point of life were to escape this material world for
spiritual union with the One, did veneration or care for the
earth really matter at all? Or did Roman imperial expansion
in the quest for more grain, an expansion that led to control
over agricultural centers throughout the empire, contribute to
environmental debasement? "The Romans failed to engage in
sustainable forms of agriculture," writes Ashley Dawson,
"seeking instead to expand their way out of ecological crisis;
the arid conditions that prevail across much of [the Mediter-
ranean] today are testaments to their improvident and destructive approach to the natural world."[7]

Environmental Degradation

What, then, were elements in this "improvident" approach?
"Here, where Rome, the capital of the world, now stands, there
once were trees and grass," wrote Ovid.[8] Unbeknownst to the
modern visitor, Rome's seven hills were once covered with
dense forests. Dionysius of Halicarnassus described the Aventine as a hill filled with trees and beautiful laurels that had
been cut down and replaced by buildings of every sort. The
Caelian Hill, to the northeast of the Aventine, was first called
the *Mons Querquetulanus*, or Oak Hill, while the Viminal to the
north of the Caelian was named after the willow tree groves

---

[7] Ashley Dawson, *Extinction: A Radical History* (New York: OR Books, 2016),
32–33.
[8] Ovid, *Fasti* 2.93–94.

that covered it. As the empire expanded, urbanization increased; imperial Rome either developed existing towns or built imperial cities in its many colonies as centers of military authority and economic control over the agricultural, timber, and mineral riches within its colonies: "After military conquest, the imperial program was Romanization by urbanization for commercialization."[9] Colonial urbanization throughout the empire was built, in part, upon deforestation. In turn, the result of cutting down heavily forested areas was "serious erosion that washed away the rich deep soil and consequently dried up the springs and streams that formerly existed. . . . The forests were exhausted for the construction of buildings and villas of 'Persian' magnificence."[10]

Not only were forests leveled for the sake of building cities, but deforestation was accelerated by the need to create room for ever-expanding agricultural work (with no grain, there was no bread, and with no bread, there were urban riots). By the third century CE, "it is likely that no extensive forest remained in the plains or low hills surrounding the Mediterranean."[11] With deforestation throughout the empire, environmental disasters emerged incrementally: the loss of vegetative cover that once served as protection against soil erosion, increased flooding—well known but little understood—due to the loss of rain-absorbing plant life that once flourished in the midst of forests along river banks, and siltation of once-fresh water sources. With the accumulation of water in lowlands, marshes—a breeding ground for armies of mosquitoes that brought malaria to imperial cities—emerged. Due to open

---

[9] John Dominic Crossan, *God and Empire: Jesus Against Rome, Then and Now* (New York: HarperOne, 2007), 13.

[10] Hughes, *Environmental Problems*, 68. Let me note here that this claim is a contentious one. See Richard Hoffmann, *An Environmental History of Medieval Europe* (New York: Cambridge University Press, 2014), 36–37.

[11] John R. McNeil, *The Mountains of the Mediterranean: An Environmental History* (Cambridge: Cambridge University Press, 1992), 72–73.

sewers, animal excrement, and most of the population crowded into *insulae*, or "tenements," cities were "smothered in flies, mosquitoes, and other insects that flourish where there is much stagnant water and exposed filth. And, like bad odors, insects are very democratic."[12]

Perhaps one of the most devastating forces that contributed to environmental degradation was armed conflict. Let us be clear: while Caesar Augustus was hailed as the great bringer of peace, such "peace" was frequently accomplished through the exercise of violent military force. Nations and tribes were colonized with the threat of armed action should they balk at Rome's takeover of their land and economy. A case in point is Roman Palestine. In 66 CE, some thirty years after the death of Jesus, an armed revolt against Roman imperial control and its oppressive tax system prompted the emperor, Nero, to dispatch his general Vespasian to crush the uprising. Joined by his son Titus, Vespasian led some sixty thousand soldiers in first "pacifying"—destroying—rebel strongholds in Galilee. One estimate suggests that thousands of Galileans were murdered by the advancing force. Titus then moved south to Judea and, in 69 CE, to Jerusalem, the rebel stronghold. The initial Roman attack on the city's defenders was a humiliating loss, as orchards, gardens, groves of trees, and hedges hid the highly mobile Judean warriors who exacted heavy casualties on the Roman infantry. In turn, low-ranking imperial soldiers and slaves were then ordered to destroy the trees and vegetation and level the ground to make for an easier approach to the city walls. In order to breach the walls of the city, Titus ordered all trees outside the walls to be cut down for the construction of battering rams. Having broken through the gates, the Romans encountered fierce resistance and then cut down more trees

---

[12] Rodney Stark, *The Rise of Christianity: How the Obscure, Marginal Jesus Movement Became the Dominant Religious Force in the Western World in a Few Centuries* (San Francisco: HarperSanFrancisco, 1997), 153.

far beyond the city in order to construct siege towers. In his narration of the revolt, the Romano-Jewish commentator Josephus wrote that "those places which were adorned with trees and pleasant gardens had now become desolate country; all its trees were cut down. Nor could any foreigner that had formerly seen Judaea and the most beautiful suburbs of the city recognize it now: it had become a desert."[13] The eventual defeat of the Judean force brought considerable damage to the city's water sources. The surrounding region was bereft of any agriculture that could sustain the survivors; the Roman army had confiscated or destroyed the farmland.

The military campaigns of imperial Rome were little different from those of other empires; deliberate destruction of land, crops, forests, and water sources was a tangible and horrific form of public propaganda. Environmental warfare was intended to make clear that revolt would risk the death of people, arable land, and water sources so that any thought of resistance to imperial control among future generations would quickly die. "The threat of war was often [harmful to] the countryside; farm families were killed, their properties requisitioned by the troops, their crops, buildings, and terraces destroyed. The reliefs of Trajan's Column [113 CE in Rome] show soldiers setting fire to villages and rounding up peasants as prisoners and slaves."[14]

While Roman imperial poets hailed the emperor as *pacifer* ("the peace bringer"), his "peace" was the result of silencing colonial voices critical of their subjugation, suppressing revolt

---

[13] Josephus, *The Jewish War* 6.1.1.

[14] Hughes, *Environmental Problems,* 154. I note here what I have not discussed of Roman environmental degradation: the link between deforestation for the sake of overgrazing and consequent soil erosion; air pollution due to the open burning of wood products; intentional setting of fire to crops, forests, and cities as a weapon of war; scarring and exhaustion of the land due to intense mining; the poisoning of waterways with lead, arsenic, and mercury from mining projects; and the killing of wild animals in enormous numbers during the games.

with deadly force, and destroying the land so that nothing might grow to support those who resisted living in his kingdom. "Rome's exploitation of the entire world [and] its enslavement of both humans and nature by violent military conquest" were palpable expressions of the thirst for domination over the many by the few.[15] No wonder Jesus' proclamation of a different kingdom, the kingdom of God—a proclamation that led to his death at the hands of Rome's "divine" injustice—was met with praise by some and rejection by others.

Resistance Poetics

The author of the Gospel of Luke narrates the well-known story of Jesus' birth in Bethlehem, a birth that is announced by angelic messengers to a group of frightened shepherds.

> [A]n angel of the Lord stood before them, and the glory of the Lord shone around them, and they were terrified. But the angel said to them, "Do not be afraid; for see—I am bringing you good news of great joy for all the people: to you is born this day in the city of David a *Savior*, who is [Christ], the *Lord*. . . . And suddenly there was with the angel a multitude of the heavenly host, praising God and saying,
>
> > "*Glory to God* in the highest heaven,
> >   and *on earth peace* among those whom he favors!"[16]

At first glance, the story is so familiar that its disruptive nature might not be readily discerned. Yet within the context of imperial Rome and Rome's emperor, its presentation of an *alternative* to Rome's way of life would have been shocking to

---

[15] Barbara Rossing, "Alas for the Earth! Lament and Resistance in Revelation 12," in *The Earth Story in the New Testament*, ed. Norman Habel and Vicky Balabanski (London: Sheffield Academic Press, 2002), 191.

[16] Luke 2:9-11, 13-14; emphasis mine.

those who read the story in the first century—for when the angels sing "Glory to God in the highest heaven, / and on earth peace among those whom he favors," when they announce that a Savior and Lord is born in a colonized town, they are not simply communicating interesting information to a group of startled shepherds. They are announcing that Caesar Augustus is *not* the savior of the world. They are singing of a kingdom that is so different from the violent colonial rule of Rome, a kingdom marked by God's peace rather than empire's violence. They are singing of the advent of the reign of God, a reign *in conflict* with the reign of Caesar and of all those who imagine they have absolute control over the earth. For in that world, there could be only one savior who asks for people's loyalty.

While that song and that announcement praise God, *they do far more*: they hold the power to shape one's worldview, encouraging one to envision what is asked of those who sing the angelic hymn and answer the question "Who rules over the earth?" In a society that hailed the emperor as the savior of the world, the angel announced the birth of a rival to that Roman savior. Indeed, to encourage people to sing of God's glory was to direct praise away from anyone who claimed themselves worthy of being its sole recipient. There is the Sacred Majesty, the emperor and his control over the lands of an expanding empire, and there is God in the highest heaven, who desires peace on earth. In this pairing, God and earth, theology and ecology, can be distinguished but not separated. In effect, the birth narrative holds a subversive quality within the context of Roman rule: it is not the mortal Caesar but the transcendent God who rules over the globe and calls for peace, not violence, on earth. For those of us who live some two thousand years after the birth of Jesus, it is important to remember that the angelic song and the astonishing announcement could easily be perceived as high treason in the world of empires, ancient and modern.

A reassessment of Rome's "greatness" and the advance of contextual studies has led a growing number of New Testament and early Christian scholars to view the movement Jesus founded as a particular way of living that *contrasted with* the way of living shaped by Rome and imperial ambition.[17] Jesus' way of life was expressed in his first public utterance recorded in the earliest gospel: "The kingdom of God has come near; turn and believe in the good news."[18] This was not the kingdom of Caesar, or Herod, or Tiberius, but the kingdom of God. That kingdom can be understood as an alternative to and criticism of Rome's presence in every dimension of life: economic,

[17] See, for instance, Wes Howard-Brook, *"Come Out, My People": God's Call Out of Empire in the Bible and Beyond* (Maryknoll, NY: Orbis Books, 2010); Walter Brueggemann, *Out of Babylon* (Nashville: Abingdon Press, 2010); Warren Carter, *John and Empire: Initial Explorations* (New York: T&T Clark, 2008); John Dominic Crossan, *Jesus: A Revolutionary Biography* (New York: HarperOne, 1994); Crossan, *God and Empire*; K. C. Hanson and Douglas Oakman, *Palestine in the Time of Jesus: Social Structures and Social Conflicts*, 2nd ed. (Minneapolis: Fortress Press, 2008); Richard Horsley, ed., *In the Shadow of Empire: Reclaiming the Bible as a History of Faithful Resistance* (Louisville: Westminster John Knox, 2008); Scott McKnight and Joseph Modica, eds., *Jesus Is Lord, Caesar Is Not: Evaluating Empire in New Testament Studies* (Downers Grove, IL: IVP Academic, 2013); Micah Kiel, *Apocalyptic Ecology: The Book of Revelation, the Earth, and the Future* (Collegeville, MN: Liturgical Press, 2017); Gordon Lathrop, *Holy Ground: A Liturgical Cosmology* (Minneapolis: Fortress Press, 2003); Thomas F. Mathews, SJ, *The Clash of Gods: A Reinterpretation of Early Christian Art* (Princeton: Princeton University Press, 1993); Douglas Oakman, *The Political Aims of Jesus* (Minneapolis: Fortress Press, 2012); Richard Horsley, ed., *Paul and Politics: Ekklesia, Israel, Imperium, Interpretations; Essays in Honor of Krister Stendahl* (Harrisburg, PA: Trinity Press International, 2000); Barbara Rossing, *The Rapture Exposed: The Message of Hope in the Book of Revelation* (New York: Basic Books, 2005); Graydon Snyder, *Ante Pacem: Archaeological Evidence of Church Life before Constantine*, rev. ed. (Macon, GA: Mercer University Press, 2003); Graydon Snyder, *Inculturation of the Jesus Tradition: The Impact of Jesus on Jewish and Roman Cultures* (Harrisburg, PA: Trinity Press International, 1999); Walter Wink, *The Powers That Be: Theology for a New Millennium* (Minneapolis: Augsburg Fortress, 1998).

[18] Mark 1:15; translation mine. I do not follow the King James translation of *metanoeite* as "repent" but rather translate it as "change your minds," "move in a new direction," or "reform your lives."

environmental, political, religious, and social.[19] Jesus' proclamation raised and raises a fundamental question: Who or what rules your life? The answer to that question, then and now, could spell the difference between conformity to cultural norms and calling them into question. Indeed, to call into question Rome's "greatness" and its rule throughout every dimension of life was to question the authority of the gods and the gods' anointed agent: the emperor.

One promising strain in biblical interpretation suggests that the communities in which the New Testament writings came to life were well aware of the environmental, political, and social context in which they worshiped the God revealed in Jesus Christ. That awareness was frequently expressed in the psalms, acclamations, canticles, and hymns sung in the early Christian liturgy. In his study of these poetic texts, Matthew Gordley notes that biblical lyrics not only communicate praise or petition to God; they serve, more importantly, a didactic or formative function in the community singing them: "They offer a way of viewing the world, a way of understanding the community's present circumstances, and at times, a desirable set of responses to those circumstances."[20]

In addition to their didactic or formative function, biblical lyrics "show an implicit, and at times, explicit, concern for *resistance* to other grand narratives about reality that may have a claim on the lives of community members."[21] These lyrics

---

[19] I recognize that the gospels and the other New Testament writings are symbolic texts and thus hold a variety of meanings; they cannot be reduced to one meaning. The two-thousand-year history of interpretation alone supports such a claim. But along with other historians, I *do* claim that the economic, environmental, and political dimensions of the text need consideration and can reveal different and sometimes surprising perspectives that may well alter one's interpretation of the text.

[20] Matthew E. Gordley, *New Testament Christological Hymns: Exploring Texts, Contexts, and Significance* (Downers Grove, IL: IVP Academic, 2018), 67.

[21] Gordley, *New Testament Christological Hymns*, 67; emphasis mine.

thus formed a genre of literature known as *resistance poetics,* texts that resisted "the project of empire" and "envisioned, advocated, and empowered resistant action."[22] Consider the imperial Roman table practice at which invited free males (frequently, business "clients" of a "patron" who served as host) would end the meal with toasts and hymns sung in honor of the emperor and the gods of the state.[23] To be sure, such singing was both religious and political in nature: a guest demonstrated his patriotism by singing praise to the gods of the state and the deified emperor. By way of contrast, early Christians sang in praise of the One whose name is *above* every other name:

> Let each of you look not to your own interests, but to the interests of others. Let the same mind be in you that was in Christ Jesus,
>> who, though he was in the form of God,
>>> did not regard equality with God
>>> as something to be exploited,
>> but emptied himself,
>>> taking the form of a slave,
>>> being born in human likeness.
>> And being found in human form,
>>> he humbled himself
>>> and became obedient to the point of death—
>>> even death on a cross.
>> Therefore God also highly exalted him
>>> and gave him the name
>>> that is above every name,
>> so that at the name of Jesus
>>> every knee should bend,
>>> in heaven and on earth and under the earth,

[22] Gordley, *New Testament Christological Hymns,* 67–68.

[23] Dennis Smith, "The Greco-Roman Banquet," in *From Symposium to Eucharist: The Banquet in the Early Christian World* (Minneapolis: Fortress Press, 2009), 13–46.

> and every tongue should confess
> that Jesus Christ is Lord,
> to the glory of God the Father.[24]

The assertions in the text are remarkable when placed next to imperial theology. One wonders if a Roman citizen could ever have viewed a colonized peasant who was executed by the imperial guard as a figure worthy of worship or loyalty. Would such a suggestion not invite incredulity? That the hymn praises someone who emptied himself into the debased form of a slave would leave members of a status-conscious empire flabbergasted. This was a society that relied on slave labor, a highly stratified society that abhorred the thought of downward mobility and the subsequent loss of an honorable reputation. The Romans employed crucifixion, a brutal form of capital punishment that was intended to strike fear in the many who watched the crucified die an agonizing death. The cross was used to silence the victim and obliterate the memory of the person executed. It was an instrument of state terror.

Gordley and others suggest that the hymn resists the claims and values of such an empire. In counterpoint to the declaration made in Luke's birth narrative, the One crucified by Rome was acclaimed Lord—*the only one* worthy of worship. Here the emperor's authority as *dominus* of land and sea was starkly rejected. While the Roman emperor was praised in song at the Roman table, Christians resisted that claim, that ruler, and that deathly imperial worldview. In turn, they sang of the One who abandoned the privilege of being equal to God and emptied himself into human life, taking on the most debased form of that life *as a slave, as a servant*: a condition that possessed few if any legal protections, a condition exploited in Roman society. It is the servant who is worthy of praise and honor.

---

[24] Philippians 2:4-11.

Furthermore, the hymn placed at its center the powerful Roman symbol of domination—the cross—as something to be remembered, not forgotten. One can only imagine the profound skepticism regarding the memorializing of what imperial society viewed as a shameful form of death. It should come as no surprise, then, that Romans would mock any exaltation of crucifixion and be horrified to see a crucifix in a place of worship. Consider the *graffito blasfemo* found in the college of the imperial pages on the Palatine Hill in Rome, dating from 200 CE. Scratched in the wall's plaster is the image of a young man worshiping before a cross: the crucified figure—while depicted as a human body—has the head of a donkey. The inscription below the cross, written in Greek, reads *Alexamenos cebete theon*—that is, "Alexamenos worships his god."[25]

By holding the crucifixion central to the hymn, Roman notions of what is honorable and worthy of emulation were turned upside down. It is the One who lived and lives among the lowly and colonized of empire and who poured out his life in service among them who is the Lord. Thus, to sing the hymn was to resist imperial power and recognize that the term "lord" had been *redefined* by the life of Jesus, who emptied himself and became humble—that is, *humus* ("of the earth," "down to earth," "rejecting the temptation to be puffed up, arrogant," "not rising above others").[26]

If we find resistance to the authority of the emperor in the angel's announcement, in the acclamation "Jesus is Lord," and in the kenotic hymn of the Philippian community, early

---

[25] See Mathews, "The Chariot and the Donkey," in *The Clash of Gods*, 23–53; Paul Steels, CSSR, "Graffiti," in *The New Catholic Encyclopedia*, ed. William McDonald, vol. 3 (New York: McGraw Hill, 1967), 688–89; Henri LeClercq, "Graffites," in *Dictionnaire d'archéologie chrétienne et de liturgie*, ed. Fernand Cabrol and Henri LeClercq, vol. 6.2, *Gothicum—Hypsistariens* (Paris: Librairie Letouzey et Ane, 1925), 1453–542.

[26] Robert Claiborne, *The Roots of English: A Reader's Handbook of Word Origins* (New York: Times Books/Random House, 1989), 87.

Christian texts sung by adherents resisted the emperor's claim as the sole ruler over land and sea, their creatures and produce. Jewish Christ followers, familiar with the Hebrew Scriptures, would grasp the confession sung in the psalm: "The earth is the Lord's and all that is in it, / the world, and those who live in it; / for he has founded it on the seas, / and established it on the rivers."[27] For Gentiles becoming Christian and familiar with imperial assertions of control over the earth, the process of conversion would no doubt include a "change of mind" or "movement in a new direction."[28] For both Jewish and Gentile Christians, acclamations, hymns, and canticles invited them to give their loyalty, their worship, to the One who transcended imperial claims.

Consider the Colossian hymn (Colossians 1:15-20), the Johannine Prologue (John 1:1-18), and the "new songs" of the Apocalypse of John (Revelation 4:1–5:14). Written with different christological accents for diverse Christian communities in the empire, they nonetheless call into question the widely held assertion of imperial authority over the earth and its natural treasures. Keep in mind this encomium concerning Caesar Augustus: "It is the birthday of the most divine Caesar which is . . . justly set on par with *the beginning of everything* in that he restored order when everything was disintegrating . . . and *gave a new look to the whole world*. . . . For that reason, one might justly take this to be *the beginning of life and living*."[29] Written by the proconsul of Roman Asia, the letter links the birthday of the emperor with the renewal of the earth and suggests that the marking of the New Year take place on the emperor's birthday, for it was he who brought about "the

[27] Psalm 24:1-2.

[28] See n. 18.

[29] Paulus Fabius Maximus, Proconsul of Roman Asia, quoted in Frederick W. Danker, *Benefactor: Epigraphic Study of a Graeco-Roman and New Testament Semantic Field* (St. Louis: Clayton Publishing, 1982), 215–22; emphasis mine.

beginning of life and living"—an astounding claim. By way of contrast, the letter to the Colossians speaks of Christ Jesus as "[T]he firstborn of all creation . . . in [whom] all things in heaven and on earth were created, things visible and invisible, whether thrones or dominions or rulers or powers—all things have been created through him and for him."[30] Although the proconsul's declaration associated the emperor—a deified mortal—with earth's well-being, the Colossian hymn asserted that the "beloved Son" was present *prior* to earth's creation and the birth of the emperor; through Christ and for him, all things—land, water, vegetation, and earth's many creatures— were brought to life and are held together in him. Here the lyricist—perhaps mindful of the creating power of Wisdom[31]— declared that a transcendent force greater than any individual "marked out the foundations of the earth, . . . rejoicing in his inhabited world."[32] In effect, the hymn writer asks, "To whom do you give your praise: the emperor who presides over earth's domination or Christ the firstborn, in whom all things on earth are held together?"

The hymn prologue in the Gospel of John offers a similar claim: no human being brings earth into existence or gives it a "new look"; it is the preexistent Word who creates and continually sustains all things. Here the lyricist invokes the Genesis narratives that speak of a transcendent creator and divine ruler (Genesis 1:1), the goodness of the creation (Genesis 1:31), and the responsibility of the primal parent to cultivate earth's garden (Genesis 2:15). Where the agent of creation—the Word—is, there is life and light rather than death and darkness. Indeed, the hymn makes clear that the "darkness" cannot overcome the light. Has the lyricist thus associated "darkness" or night (and the inability to see clearly) with the fallible social

---

[30] Colossians 1:15-16.
[31] See Proverbs 8; Wisdom 7–10; Sirach 24.
[32] Proverbs 8:29, 31.

system of empire: "He was in the world . . .; yet *the world* did not know him"?[33] What some scholars find provocative in this hymn text is that the emperor—praised by imperial poets as the renewer of the earth—is not even mentioned: "[He] is not named in the prologue, but it is clear that the author of John's Gospel numbered him as a chief member of *the world* that did not recognize Jesus and as part of the darkness that attempted to extinguish the light of the Logos."[34] To place the emperor in the shadows was, in effect, to deny his alleged control over land and sea.

That the book of Revelation served as a polemic directed at the violence and injustice of empire, to say nothing of its persecution of Christians, is well known in contemporary scholarly studies. What has emerged more recently is an examination of the environmental sensibilities present in the text. In his study of Revelation's earth ethic, Micah Kiel notes that the author of the Apocalypse includes canticles that praise the Lamb of God and decry earth's degradation at the hands of the beast: "We see Roman propaganda claiming control of the universe and a variety of ways that that control was detrimental to the earth."[35] Consider the thousands of animals put to death in hundreds of arenas throughout the empire. Over nine thousand animals were killed in a period of one hundred days to mark the opening of Rome's infamous Colosseum.

Some thirty years later, Emperor Trajan held contests in which eleven thousand animals were killed in the arena.[36] Imagine, then, those hundreds of arenas (and the thousands sitting in them) in which the "sport" celebrated was the slaughter of animals. But more than a gruesome form of entertainment, the large-scale killing of animals, sponsored by the

---

[33] John 1:10; emphasis mine.
[34] Gordley, *New Testament Christological Hymns*, 177; emphasis mine.
[35] Kiel, *Apocalyptic Ecology*, 84.
[36] Kiel, *Apocalyptic Ecology*, 69.

emperor and supported by wealthy elites, was "a symbol of their complete power over the universe."[37] Domination of human beings through colonization, slavery, and deathly spectacles in the arena; domination of land, forests, waterways, and agriculture; and domination of animals expressed Rome's desire to control all dimensions of life. Was John not right in depicting this "domination system" as a beast with a voracious appetite?

In contrast to this deathly spectacle sponsored in the arena, the author of Revelation includes texts that offer a quite different view. Catholics and many other Christians are familiar with the canticle sung in the midst of the Eucharistic Prayer: "Holy, Holy, Holy Lord God of hosts. Heaven and earth are full of your glory. Hosanna in the highest. Blessed is he who comes in the name of the Lord. Hosanna in the highest."[38] The first part of the canticle appears in Revelation:

> The four living creatures, each of them with six wings, are full of eyes all around and inside. Day and night without ceasing they sing,
>
> > "Holy, holy, holy,
> > the Lord God the Almighty,
> > who was and is and is to come."[39]

What catches one's attention is that the canticle is led not by a chorus of human beings but rather by four living beings—a lion, an ox, an eagle, and a being with a human face—portrayed as cherubim.[40] Each creature is "full of eyes all around

---

[37] Roland Auguet, *Cruelty and Civilization: The Roman Games* (New York: Routledge, 1994), 111–12.

[38] *The Roman Missal* (2011), 384.

[39] Revelation 4:8.

[40] See Ezekiel 1:18 and 10:12, where the same four beings are listed, but in a different order.

and inside,"[41] indicating that nothing escapes their vision, that they are watchful and intelligent. In contrast to Rome's destruction of animals as objects of deadly sport, in God's realm they lead the chorus of praise: "The four living creatures that hover around the throne *supplant* human figures. John's depiction here of the heavenly realm, where all is as it should be, is noticeably nonanthropocentric; the 'human has no privilege or precedent.'"[42] The canticle and those who lead it thus serve as a "counter-ideology" to imperial domination over earth's creatures. In Caesar's kingdom, animals are slaughtered; in God's kingdom, animals live and sing praise.

The theme heard in Colossians 1 and John 1 occurs again in the second canticle, led by the twenty-four elders. Prostrate before the throne of God, they cry out, "You are worthy, our Lord and God, / to receive glory and honor and power, / for you created all things, / and by your will they existed and were created."[43] In John's polemic against empire, it is not the emperor and his supportive elites who control the vast realm of animals but rather the Creator of heaven and earth, who desires peace rather than brutal domination. This concern for earth's creatures is then expanded in a subsequent canticle:

> I heard *every creature in heaven and on earth and under the earth and in the sea*, and all that is in them, singing,
>
>> "To the one seated on the throne and to the Lamb
>> be blessing and honor and glory and might
>> forever and ever!"[44]

Here the canticle serves as a counterpoint to those psalms in which praise is offered by every creature on the earth:

[41] Revelation 4:8.

[42] Kiel, *Apocalyptic Ecology*, 75; emphasis mine.

[43] Revelation 4:10-11.

[44] Revelation 5:13; emphasis mine.

Praise the Lord from the earth,
>   you sea monsters and all deeps,
fire and hail, snow and frost. . . .

Mountains and all hills,
>   fruit trees and all cedars!
Wild animals and all cattle,
>   creeping things and flying birds!

Kings of the earth and all peoples, . . .
Young men and women alike,
>   old and young together![45]

At the same time, the Revelation canticle invokes the litany of creation in Genesis 1. That the lyricist speaks of creatures in heaven, on earth, under the earth, and in the sea draws together all creatures into the realm of the Sovereign God; their origin and their living issue forth from the Creator's provident hand. Here the nonhuman creation leads in praising the wounded yet living Lamb. And yet, as we have seen before, praise is directed to one and denied to the other who demanded it. In this one verse, we hear denunciation of the imperial deceiver.

Do we know if these acclamations, hymns, and canticles were sung in early Christian communities? There seems to be no agreement on this question. Some scholars argue that evidence of lyrics does not confirm their use in worship; they could be nothing more than imaginative compositions by the author of a gospel, a letter, or the apocalypse. Others suggest that many of them were used in some form of worship and were then quoted by New Testament authors. Still others claim that these liturgical texts, if not sung, were at least reflective of worship practices within such communities. There is agreement, however, that the very reading of "resistance poetry" within early Christian worship would inform the assembly's

---

[45] Psalm 148:7-12.

distinctive Christian identity as a minority community within the dominant imperial culture.

Earth's Gifts in Early Christian Worship

Keep in mind that early Christian communities used "living water" to wash people into the Christian community. They smeared fragrant olive oil on the bodies of the newly baptized. We read of a cup filled with milk and mixed with honey offered to the newly baptized who had entered the "promised land." Bread and wine, grain of the field and grape of the vine, were brought to the eucharistic table, where thanksgiving was made before the people received the eucharistic gifts. It would seem that the "mysteries," the sacraments, could not exist without the gifts of the earth.

Indeed, it was in this ancient Christian assembly that these images, drawn from the creation, were employed to speak of Jesus Christ and, at times, his community of followers: light in the darkness of night,[46] a dawning light for the nations,[47] the light of the world,[48] a radiant morning star,[49] the sun of

[46] "The light shines in the darkness, and the darkness did not overcome it" (John 1:5).

[47] "By the tender mercy of our God, / the dawn from on high will break upon us, / to give light to those who sit in darkness and in the shadow of death, / to guide our feet into the way of peace" (Luke 1:78-79).

[48] "I am the light of the world. Whoever follows me will never walk in darkness but will have the light of life" (John 8:12); "You are the light of the world. A city built on a hill cannot be hid. No one after lighting a lamp puts it under the bushel basket, but on the lampstand, and it gives light to all in the house. In the same way, let your light shine before others, so that they may see your good works and give glory to your Father in heaven" (Matthew 5:14-16); "Live as children of light" (Ephesians 5:8).

[49] "It is I, Jesus, who sent my angel to you with this testimony for the churches. I am . . . the bright morning star" (Revelation 22:16).

resurrection,[50] the firstborn of all creation,[51] the lamb,[52] sheep,[53] the great fish and many little fish,[54] dolphins,[55] peacocks,[56] a

[50] "He is the sun of resurrection, born before the morning star. He gives life by his rays" (Ephesians 5:14, as quoted in Clement of Alexandria, *Protrepticus* [*Exhortation to the Heathen*] IX, 84.2).

[51] "He is the image of the invisible God, the firstborn of all creation" (Colossians 1:15).

[52] "Here is the Lamb of God who takes away the sin of the world" (John 1:29); "[T]he four living creatures and the twenty-four elders fell before the Lamb, each holding a harp and golden bowls full of incense" (Revelation 5:8); concerning the image of the lamb in early Christian art, see Robin Jensen, *Understanding Early Christian Art* (London: Routledge, 2000), 141–47.

[53] "I am the good shepherd. The good shepherd lays down his life for the sheep" (John 10:11); "Then the king will say to [the sheep] at his right hand, 'Come, you that are blessed by my Father, inherit the kingdom prepared for you from the foundation of the world; for I was hungry and you gave me food, I was thirsty and you gave me something to drink, I was a stranger and you welcomed me, I was naked and you gave me clothing, I was sick and you took care of me, I was in prison and you visited me'" (Matthew 25:34-36); concerning the shepherd in early Christian art, see Snyder, *Inculturation of the Jesus Tradition*, 97–98; Susan Bratton, *Environmental Values in Christian Art* (Albany: State University of New York Press, 2008), 9–36.

[54] "[Jesus] said to them, 'Follow me, and I will make you fish for people'" (Matthew 4:19); "Fisher of people, you, their Savior, from the sea of evil you pull the pure fish; out of the hostile storm, you draw them into the life of blessedness" (Clement of Alexandria, *The Teacher* III, Hymn); "We are little fishes and Jesus Christ is our Great Fish; like fish, we in water receive our new birth" (Tertullian, *On Baptism* 1); concerning the fish image in early Christian art, see Snyder, *Inculturation of the Jesus Tradition*, 94–95, 143–45.

[55] "You dolphins and all water creatures, bless the Lord; praise and exalt him above all forever" (Song of the Three Young Men, 57); concerning the dolphin image in the Catacomb of San Callisto, Rome, see Orazio Marucchi, "Cross," in *The Catholic Encyclopedia*, ed. Charles Herbermann, vol. 4 (New York: Robert Appleton, 1908), 527.

[56] On the early Christian use of the peacock, see Peter and Linda Murray, *The Oxford Dictionary of Christian Art*, rev. ed. (Oxford: Oxford University Press, 2013), 64–65; concerning the arcosolium of the peacock in the Catacomb of Priscilla, Rome, see Sandro Carletti, *The Catacombs of Priscilla*, trans. Alice Mulhern (Vatican City: Pontifical Commission for Sacred Archaeology, 1982), 34–37.

phoenix,[57] thirst-quenching water,[58] a seed in the dark earth,[59] the bread of life,[60] the living vine,[61] flowing wine,[62] cow's milk,[63]

[57] "Let us consider that wonderful sign of the resurrection . . . a certain bird which is called a phoenix. . . . When the time of its dissolution draws near, it builds itself a nest of frankincense, myrrh, and other spices, into which it enters and dies. But as the flesh decays a new creation is born and grows. When its strength is sufficient, it takes wing in the sight all people" (Clement of Rome, *Letter to the Corinthians*, 25).

[58] "On the last day of the festival, the great day, while Jesus was standing there, he cried out, 'Let anyone who is thirsty come to me, and let the one who believes in me drink'" (John 7:37-38).

[59] "Very truly, I tell you, unless a grain of wheat falls into the earth and dies, it remains just a single grain; but if it dies, it bears much fruit" (John 12:24); "What is sown is perishable, what is raised is imperishable. It is sown in dishonor, it is raised in glory. It is sown in weakness, it is raised in power. It is sown a physical body, it is raised a spiritual body. If there is a physical body, there is also a spiritual body" (1 Corinthians 15:42-44); concerning the seed in early Christianity, see Photina Rech, OSB, "Grain and Ear, Sowing and Reaping," in *Wine and Bread*, trans. Heinz R. Kuehn (Chicago: Liturgy Training Publications, 1998), 71–90.

[60] "Jesus said to them, 'I am the bread of life. Whoever comes to me will never be hungry'" (John 6:35); "[Jesus said to the disciples], 'You give them something to eat'" (Mark 6:37); concerning the breaking of the bread, see Jensen, *Understanding Early Christian Art*, 52–59; Rech, *Wine and Bread*, 91–112.

[61] "I am the true vine, and my Father is the vinegrower. He removes every branch in me that bears no fruit. Every branch that bears fruit he prunes to make it bear more fruit" (John 15:1-2); "We thank you, our Father, for the holy vine of David your servant which you have revealed to us through Jesus your Child" (*The Didache or Teaching of the Twelve Apostles*, 9).

[62] "[H]e took the cup also, after supper, saying, 'This cup is the new covenant in my blood. Do this, as often as you drink it, in remembrance of me'" (1 Corinthians 11:25); "A grape on the vine sustains no pressing and so nothing flows from it; yet when it is thrown into the winepress, it is pressed down. Harm seems to be done to the grape but this harm is not futile: if there were no suffering, it would have remained barren. . . . When you have begun to live in Christ and the inevitable suffering it brings, you have entered in the winepress. Make yourself ready for pressing: do not be dry but let the pressing out of good wine begin" (Augustine, *Explanation of Psalm 56*, 3–4).

[63] "Like newborn infants, long for the pure, spiritual milk, so that by it you may grow into salvation" (1 Peter 2:2); "O Christ Jesus, you are the heavenly milk pressed from the sweet breasts of a young mother, full of the graces of your wisdom. Our tender lips seek to be nourished by the spiritual

and palm branches.[64] But, then, we should not be surprised that early Christians used the things of this earth in their worship—as diverse as that worship might have been in practice—or that images drawn from the heavens and the earth spoke of the birth, life, ministry, death, and resurrection of Jesus Christ. In reading the gospels or hearing a selection from one proclaimed in the liturgy, we are frequently presented with the *materiality* of this earth present in those very gospels and thus in the life of Jesus: stars, daybreak, a setting sun, night, windstorms, scorching heat, fire, clouds, torrential rain, mud, earthquakes, the wilderness and dust, stones, hills, mountaintops, seas, a flowing river, a flooding river, lakes, springs, pools of water, trees, reeds, seeds, flowers, grass, fruit, sheep, lambs, pigs, fish, foxes, hens, a fatted calf, ravens, vultures, dogs, a colt, vines, vineyards, grapes, grainfields, olive oil, salt, figs, herbs, and spices.[65] The gospels proclaimed in the assembly presented and present the *matter* of earth and the heavens, of days and seasons, in stunning array.

---

milk" (Clement of Alexandria, *The Teacher* III, Hymn); "In my vision I saw an immense garden, and in it a silver-haired man sat in shepherd's garb milking sheep. He called me over and gave me a mouthful of the milk he was drawing; and I took it into my cupped hands and consumed it" (*The Passion of Perpetua and Felicity*, 3); concerning the image of a shepherd with a bucket of milk in early Christian catacombs, see Robin Jensen, "Milk and Honey," in *Baptismal Imagery in Early Christianity: Ritual, Visual, and Theological Dimensions* (Ada, MI: Baker Books, 2012), 122–27.

[64] "The next day the great crowd that had come to the festival heard that Jesus was coming to Jerusalem. So they took branches of palm trees and went out to meet him, shouting, // 'Hosanna! / Blessed is the one who comes in the name of the Lord— / the King of Israel!'" (John 12:12-13); "[T]here was a great multitude that no one could count . . . standing before the throne and before the Lamb, robed in white, with palm branches in their hands" (Revelation 7:9); concerning the palm in early Christian art, see Henri LeClercq, "Palme, Palmier," *DACL* 13.1 (1937): 947–61.

[65] Drawn from the Gospel of Luke.

While some historians have argued that the Christian tradition is strongly if not overwhelmingly unfriendly to the earth,[66] the presence of the earth in New Testament texts, songs and acclamations, worship, and art[67] argues differently. Gordon Lathrop suggests that the gospels as "biographical" texts are profoundly concerned about life in particular locations, in the earthy places where Christians gathered for worship, and what they welcomed from the created world into their common life.[68] One might say that much of early Christian worship was *ecophilic* (i.e., marked by a love for the things of this earth, a love shaped by Jesus, the material presence of God in the world) in contrast to the *ecophobic* spirituality promoted in the Gnostic gospels. After all, Christians worshiped a human being who was tortured and "suffered under Pontius Pilate" in the city of Jerusalem during the annual celebration of God's liberation of the Hebrews from another oppressive imperial power—a celebration that included lamb, bread, herbs, and wine and a communal, domestic liturgy that was scheduled according to the appearance of the full moon in the spring. They did not worship a spirit or *aeon* who transcended time and place. Indeed, at the heart of Christian faith and life was the conviction that the risen Christ, "the first fruits" of creation,[69] was present to the assembly through the gifts of the

---

[66] Lynn T. White Jr., "The Historical Roots of Our Ecologic Crisis," *Science* 155.3767 (1967): 1203–7. White claimed that Christianity is the primary source of ecological degradation in the West, a claim made, surprisingly, with no evidence. Nonetheless, his claim has fed other cultural and environmental historians who have used selective evidence (e.g., a noncontextual reading of Revelation, occasional quotations from Augustine) to suggest that the Christian tradition is essentially an ecophobic religion destructive of the earth.

[67] Chapters 2–4 in Bratton's *Environmental Values* discusses the portrayal of Christ as the agent of creation and the supervisor of the four seasons; the role of vines, plants, trees, and flowers; and the presence of birds, fish, and animals in early Christian art.

[68] Lathrop, *Holy Ground*, 128–36.

[69] 1 Corinthians 15:23.

created world. What did one of the earliest eucharistic thanksgivings say? "Now concerning the Eucharist, give thanks this way. First, concerning the cup: 'We thank you, our Father, for the holy vine of David your servant which you have revealed to us through Jesus, your Child. . . . You created all things for your name's sake, and you have given food and drink to humankind for their enjoyment.'"[70]

What is proclaimed in this thanksgiving? There is only one who is the beginning of life and living, and that One is not the emperor. That One, the Creator, is revealed, made matter, in the holy vine of Jesus. From that One there flows forth the gifts of the earth (signified in food and drink), sustaining life and bringing joy. Flowing water; scented oil; loaves of bread; amphorae of wine, honey, and milk; gathering at dawn and singing at sunset: there seems to be no disembodied, earth-transcending spirituality here (though the Neoplatonic temptation was never far from the Christian imagination). Rather, it was the wounded yet living Lamb, the firstborn of all creation, the life and the light of all people, who captured the imagination of Christians with his earth-embracing materiality, what would come to be called the Mystery of the Incarnation.

[70] *Didache,* 9.

2

Benedict's Journey
Out of Imperial
Christianity

During the annual festival of Passover, the commemoration of Hebrew slaves being freed from imperial Egypt,[1] Jesus of Nazareth was put to death by crucifixion, nailed by hands and feet to a cross—a form of capital punishment the Romans borrowed from Persia.[2] Those who opposed his commitment to the reign of God thought his death would silence him and scatter the group of followers who had given him a tumultuous welcome as he entered the city of Jerusalem only a few days before.[3] Yet with his arrest on a Thursday night, many of his own disciples abandoned him, hiding themselves in apartments throughout the city. As a grisly form of imperial propaganda, public crucifixion along main roads outside city gates was intended to strike fear in those who contemplated criticism in word or deed of Rome's power. The Gospel of Mark, the earliest gospel written, notes that after Jesus died, a man named Joseph of Arimathea gained permission to take the body and place it in a tomb hewn out of rock, the opening sealed with a large stone.[4] One might well imagine

[1] Exodus 1–15; Psalm 78.
[2] Mark 15:15-47; Matthew 27:26-66; Luke 23:24-56; John 19:16-42.
[3] Mark 11:1-11; Matthew 21:1-11; Luke 19:28-44; John 12:12-19.
[4] Mark 15:42-47.

that Pontius Pilate, the Roman governor who had ordered Jesus' execution, and the Roman soldiers who had witnessed his death would conclude: "His movement now ends."

Yet such was not the case. The writers of the gospels and letters that would come to be called the New Testament were at pains to describe what Jesus' followers experienced after his death. While contemporary Christians celebrate Easter (or Pascha[5])—the resurrection of Jesus from death—there were no witnesses to this event. According to the gospel accounts, there were only appearances of the risen Jesus to women and men who were his followers during his life or new followers after his death.[6] What interests the historian is this: Did the experience of the disciples in these encounters make any difference in their lives and the lives of people with whom they lived or met in their travels? And, if so, what did that difference look like?

Paul, the writer of the earliest Christian texts, alludes to the practices that marked early Christians. Small *communities* were formed: for example, he addresses letters "[t]o the church of the Thessalonians"[7] and "[t]o the church of God that is in Corinth."[8] These house church gatherings[9] came into existence

[5] *Pascha* is the earliest name for the holy day commemorating the resurrection, a Greek translation of the Hebrew *pesach*, or "Passover." The date of Easter, or Pascha, changes each year; it is the first Sunday after the first full moon after the spring equinox, March 21.

[6] Jesus appears to Mary Magdalene (John 20:11-18); to women disciples (Matthew 28:9-10); to Peter (Luke 24:34); to Cleopas and another disciple on the road to Emmaus during the day (Luke 24:13-31); to a group of disciples in the evening (Luke 24:36-49; John 20:19-25); to disciples, especially Thomas, a week later (John 20:26-29); to disciples fishing by the Sea of Galilee (John 21:1-13); to disciples on a mountain in Galilee (Matthew 28:16-18); to Stephen, the first martyr (Acts 7:55-56); to Paul (1 Corinthians 15:8-9); and to John, the Seer of Patmos (Revelation 1:9-19).

[7] 1 Thessalonians 1:1.

[8] 1 Corinthians 1:2.

[9] At first, the early Christians, or Christ followers, met in houses or apartments. As they grew in numbers, Christian communities renovated homes

through the persuasive speaking and actions of mobile Christian leaders, sometimes called *apostles* ("those who are sent"; "Paul, a servant of Jesus Christ, called to be an apostle";[10] "Andronicus and Junia, . . . prominent among the apostles"[11]), who communicated a new way of life rooted in the words and deeds of Jesus. Within a highly stratified society, the Christian community was marked by an *equality* bestowed through its initiation practice: "As many of you as were baptized into Christ have clothed yourselves with Christ. There is no longer Jew or Greek, there is no longer slave or free, there is no longer male and female; for all of you are one in Christ Jesus."[12]

Early Christians gathered at table on Sunday, a workday, for "the Lord's supper,"[13] "the breaking of bread,"[14] what would come to be called the *Eucharist* ("thanksgiving"), the *Mass* ("being sent"), or the Holy Communion: a meal ritual that continued the inclusive meal practice of Jesus in which thanks was given to God over bread and then over wine, the bread was broken apart and eaten by all present, a supper was eaten, and then thanks was given to God over a cup of wine, from which each person drank. Here the relationship between the actions of the supper and the life of Jesus became apparent: his life was "broken open" to others, "poured out" in passion for the reign of God: "For as often as you eat this bread and drink the cup, you proclaim the Lord's death until he comes."[15] Paul castigated the factionalism among Christians in Corinth that led to the wealthy eating a sumptuous meal during the Supper, leaving nothing for poor workers who arrived late.

---

or rented larger meeting spaces; see Graydon Snyder, *Ante Pacem: Archaeological Evidence of Church Life Before Constantine*, rev. ed. (Macon, GA: Mercer University Press, 2013), 128–209.

[10] Romans 1:1.

[11] Romans 16:7.

[12] Galatians 3:27-28.

[13] 1 Corinthians 11:20.

[14] Acts 2:42.

[15] 1 Corinthians 11:26.

This is not the Lord's Supper, he admonished them, in light of Jesus' *meal practice*; Jesus shared food and drink across socio-economic boundaries of gender, class, and race, a meal practice that gained him both criticism and praise.

The author of the letter of James gave advice for those who were ill: "Are any among you sick? They should call for the elders of the church and have them pray over them, anointing them with oil in the name of the Lord. The prayer of faith will save the sick, and the Lord will raise them up."[16] This ritual practice was one way in which early Christians continued the *healing practice* of Jesus. At the same time, early Christians offered rudimentary medical care to the sick and dying. Tertullian, an African Christian, wrote that "though we have our treasure chest, it is not made up of membership dues as if we are a religion that charges people to join. Rather, if one is able, each person offers a donation. There is no compulsion here for all is voluntary. . . . These gifts are used to assist and bury the poor, care for impoverished orphans and the elderly who are ill and homebound."[17] In Rome, the Christian convert Justin Martyr wrote that "they who are well to do, and willing, give what each thinks fit; and what is collected is deposited with the president,[18] who cares for orphans and widows and those who, through sickness or any other cause, are in want."[19]

In a patriarchal society ruled by men, Paul praised *women leaders* among Christians: "I commend to you our sister *Phoebe*, a *deacon* of the church at Cenchreae. . . . Greet *Prisca* and Aquila, who work with me in Christ Jesus. . . . Greet *Mary*, who has worked very hard among you. Greet Andronicus and *Junia*, . . . who . . . are prominent among the *apostles*."[20] There

[16] James 5:14-15.

[17] *Apology* 39.

[18] Justin Martyr refers to the person who leads communal worship as the president.

[19] *First Apology* 67.

[20] Romans 16:1, 3, 6, 7; emphasis mine.

are a variety of *leaders* in the community: "God has appointed in the church first apostles, second prophets, third teachers; then deeds of power, then gifts of healing, forms of assistance, forms of leadership."[21] Later New Testament writings mention supervisors (bishops) and servers (deacons): "Keep watch over yourselves and over all the flock, of which the Holy Spirit has made you overseers, to shepherd the church of God."[22] "[W]hoever aspires to the office of bishop desires a noble task. . . . Deacons likewise . . . must hold fast to the mystery of the faith."[23]

What we encounter in these glimpses of early Christian life after the death and resurrection of Jesus is what sociologists call the process of *structuralization*: the emergence of practices that will ensure the founder's mission or message will continue into the future. Paul spoke of this movement as a living, breathing, developing body alive in the world: "[J]ust as the [human] body is one and has many members, and all the members of the body, though many, are one body, so it is with Christ. For in the one Spirit *we were all baptized into one body*—Jews or Greeks, slaves or free—and we were all made to drink of one Spirit."[24] The author of 1 Peter wrote of Christ's followers as a pilgrim people, traveling in and through this world but not assimilated into its way of life: "[Y]ou [are] *aliens and exiles*. . . . Conduct yourselves honorably among the Gentiles, so that, though they malign you as evildoers, they may see your honorable deeds and glorify God."[25] The anonymous author of the letter to Diognetus wrote in a similar vein: "Christians live in their own countries as though they were *only passing through*. They play their full role as citizens, but labor under all the disabilities of aliens. Any country can be their homeland,

----

[21] 1 Corinthians 12:28.

[22] Acts 20:28.

[23] 1 Timothy 3:1, 8-9.

[24] 1 Corinthians 12:12-13; emphasis mine.

[25] 1 Peter 2:11-12; emphasis mine.

but for them their homeland, wherever it may be, is a foreign country. Like others, they marry and have children, but they do not expose them. They share their meals, but not their wives. . . . Condemned because they are not understood, they are put to death, but raised to life again. They live in poverty, but enrich many."[26]

Rather than an established social institution, early Christians were more a movement in society; after all, the term commonly used for Christians in the New Testament is *ekklesia*, an assembly of people *called out* for a particular purpose.[27]

That purpose was marked by a distinctive *ethic of care for others*—an ethic grounded in their understanding of the life and mission of Jesus Christ. For instance, Roman law allowed a father to murder his newborn infant or expose the child to the elements and predatory animals, a practice rejected by Christians, who were known to collect newly abandoned children and raise them in what would come to be called an orphanage: "They marry and have children, but *they do not expose them.*"[28] Early Christians denounced abortion as the murder of a fetus made in the image of God as well as a practice that could easily kill the mother, so unhygienic and damaging were medical procedures.

At the beginning of the second century, Emperor Trajan banned all supper clubs and their meal practices as potential centers of sedition against the state. Christians were included in this ban, and thus the thanksgiving to God over bread and then wine with eating and drinking was retained and the actual supper or meal dropped out. But the practice of providing a meal did not disappear; rather, it became *a meal for the hungry*

---

[26] *Diognetus* V; emphasis mine.

[27] Latin *ecclesia*, "ecclesial"; see Matthew 16:18; Acts 5:11; Romans 16:1; 1 Corinthian 1:2; and 108 other instances in the New Testament. Indeed, it is this notion of a reforming movement that captured the imagination of subsequent reformers in Christian history.

[28] *Diognetus* V; emphasis mine.

poor.[29] The practice of providing a meal for people challenged by poverty was no doubt inspired by the meal practice of Jesus as well as by one of his exhortations: "When you give a luncheon or a dinner, do not invite your friends or your brothers or your relatives or rich neighbors, in case they may invite you in return, and you would be repaid. But when you give a banquet, invite the poor, the crippled, the lame, and the blind."[30] People who had limited access to food could thus rely on at least one substantial meal each week.

During the pandemics of 165 and 261—pandemics that killed millions of people in Central and Western Asia, North and East Africa, and the Mediterranean Basin—Christians sought out their neighbors who were stricken with illness and cared for children orphaned by their parents' deaths. While the famous Roman physician Galen described the plague, he fled—as did many other physicians—abandoning those who were ill and dying. According to the reports of their leaders, Christians offered rudimentary nursing care to Christian and non-Christian alike; they buried the dead who had been left in homes or piled on the streets; and, most importantly, they offered companionship to those who had been abandoned by their families and friends.[31] When asked why members of this minority group would place themselves in harm's way, one of their bishops responded that Christians had no fear of death,

[29] See Samuel Torvend, *Still Hungry at the Feast: Eucharistic Justice in the Midst of Affliction* (Collegeville, MN: Liturgical Press, 2019), 84–101; Valeriy A. Alikin, *The Earliest History of the Christian Gathering: Origin, Development and Content of the Christian Gathering in the First to Third Centuries* (Leiden and Boston: Brill, 2010), 100–102, 142–43; Adalbert Hamman, *Vie Liturgique et Vie Sociale* (Paris: Desclée & Cie, 1968), 153–260.

[30] Luke 14:12-13.

[31] See Gary Ferngren, *Medicine and Health Care in Early Christianity* (Baltimore: Johns Hopkins University Press, 2009), 62–85, 113–39; Vincenzo Monachino, *La Carità Cristiana a Roma* (Rome: Cappelli Editore, 1968); Rodney Stark, *The Rise of Christianity: How the Obscure, Marginal Jesus Movement Became the Dominant Religious Force in the Western World in a Few Centuries* (San Francisco: HarperSanFrancisco, 1997), 72–94.

for death was not the end of life. The bishop also said Christians were encouraged by the words of Jesus, who said, "This is my commandment, that you love one another as I have loved you. No one has greater love than this, to lay down one's life for one's friends."[32]

In his study of Christianity during its first centuries, the sociologist Rodney Stark described early Christianity as a "revitalization movement" that was able to mobilize its members for active engagement with social crises or issues. This was possible, he argues, because early Christians created a network of social assistance unrivaled in the ancient world, directed by a cohort of deacons and supervising bishops, and supported by the labor and donations of members.[33] It is worth remembering that there was no governmental support for citizens, other than the Roman *annona*, the offering of grain or bread to the poorest inhabitants in the capital city. There was no social security, no state-sponsored healthcare, no subsidized housing, no unemployment assistance. By way of contrast, the Christian network of social relief included care for the most vulnerable members of society: abandoned infants and young children, pregnant women, individuals and communities suffering from sickness and epidemics, the homeless, the hungry poor, widows, and unmarried women with no relatives.[34] Such structured generosity became tangible in the creation of orphanages, hospices, meal sites, housing, and food and clothing distribution centers—a generosity animated by the teaching of Jesus: "Come, you that are blessed by my Father, inherit the kingdom prepared for you from the foundation of the world; for I was hungry and you gave me food, I was thirsty and you gave me

---

[32] John 15:12-13.

[33] Stark, *Rise of Christianity*, 23–67; also Anthony Wallace, who, based on his study of a nineteenth-century Iroquois movement, coined the term in "Revitalization Movements," *American Anthropologist* 58 (1956): 264–81.

[34] See Bonnie Bowman Thurston, *Widows: A Women's Ministry in the Early Church* (Minneapolis: Fortress Press, 1989).

something to drink, I was a stranger and you welcomed me, I was naked and you gave me clothing, I was sick and you took care of me, I was in prison and you visited me."[35]

This ethic of care was promoted in Christian communities that experienced lesser or greater degrees of *cultural intolerance*: "[I]n spite of persecution you received the word with joy."[36] The last book of the Christian Scriptures, the book of Revelation, was written in light of Roman persecution; Christians were thought to be atheists (they did not believe in the many gods of Rome) and unpatriotic (they did not worship the gods of the state or the emperor at public festivals). In the year 112, Pliny the Younger, a governor in Roman Asia (modern-day Turkey), wrote to Emperor Trajan concerning his experience with Christians.

> I have taken this course about those who have been brought before me as Christians. I asked them whether they were Christians or not. If they confessed that they were Christians, I asked them again, and a third time, intermixing threats with the questions. If they persevered in their confession, I ordered them to be executed; for I did not doubt . . . their inflexible obstinacy . . . in this mad sect. . . . Others accused of being Christian denied it. . . . They worshipped your image, and the images of our gods; they also cursed Christ.[37]

What did Pliny discover in his examination of Christians, including two women deacons? They met on a particular day (Sunday?) before dawn and sang a hymn to Christ. They vowed in a *sacramentum* to do no wrong to others. They held an innocent meal. All this Pliny referred to as a "superstition" and a "contagion" that had spread from cities to towns to rural

---

[35] Matthew 25:34-36.
[36] 1 Thessalonians 1:6.
[37] *Letters* X.96.

areas and counts many "of every age, of every rank, and of both sexes."[38]

As the witness of Pliny makes clear, the Christian movement, a minority group within Roman imperial society, was viewed with annoyance, skepticism, intolerance, and even sporadic persecution. Christian refusal to worship the emperor's image and the images of the gods, and their refusal to support local markets by purchasing incense, grain, or animals for sacrifice to the gods, was met with questioning, arrest, imprisonment, or death. Their absence from public festivals in honor of Rome and its divine benefactors had become obvious. And their failure to perform this "patriotic" duty made them easy targets when disaster befell the state. If only these "atheists" had worshipped the gods, said their critics, this disaster would not have occurred.

Contemporary historical studies reveal that a small number of Christians were put to death in public for their refusal to deny their allegiance to Jesus Christ—a clear rebuke of the emperor's claim to be lord over all creation and the savior of the world. Christian martyrs were considered heroic in their attitude toward death at the hands of gladiators or wild animals. The first extant document written by a Christian woman is the martyr diary of a young African named Perpetua. Arrested in 203 CE for her entrance into the Christian faith through baptism and her refusal to deny her new identity, she was sent to the arena to be executed. The writer who completed her diary observed this: "The Christians went to the spot [in the arena] of their own accord as the spectators wanted them to. The martyrs kissed one another, sealing their deaths with the ritual kiss of peace. They took the sword in silence and without moving. . . . Perpetua was struck on the bone by the gladiator and let out a cry; then she took the trembling hand of the young gladiator and guided his sword to her throat.

[38] *Letters* X.96.

It was as though so great a woman could not be put to death unless she herself were willing."[39]

There is no evidence that thousands of Christians were martyred. Rather, there were thousands, if not tens of thousands, of people *watching*, and many admiring, those who were put to death because of their allegiance to Jesus, the first martyr. Indeed, the Christian gospels narrate the arrest of Jesus and his trial before a hostile governmental tribunal, an experience shared by early Christians who were arrested and those who became Christian martyrs.

Imperialization of the Christian Movement

One hundred years after the death of Perpetua and her companions, Emperor Diocletian commanded his guard to cut out the tongue of a Christian deacon named Romanus because he had interrupted sacrifices being made to the gods. A few days later, the deacon was executed. Not long after Romanus's death, Diocletian was convinced by his court that substantial and widespread measures needed to be taken against the growing number of Christians throughout the empire: only debilitating action would appease the Roman gods and guarantee the success of the army in its attempts to defend the borders from invasion.

Beginning on February 24, 303, Diocletian published a series of edicts against Christians, ordering the destruction of their Scriptures and places of worship, prohibiting their gathering for worship, ordering the arrest of Christian leaders, and demanding that all Christians make sacrifices to the Roman gods upon pain of execution if they refused.

By 305, the imperial bureaucracy had been purged of Christians, many Christian leaders had been arrested and exiled or

---

[39] *Passion of Perpetua and Felicity*, 20.

executed, and Christian assemblies had been disbanded. In that same year, Diocletian resigned thinking that governmental persecution had suppressed what Pliny had once called a growing "contagion." But such was not the case. A resilient Christian movement was able to provide a continuing stream of leadership from the ground up and maintain its service to those in need of social assistance.

What has been called the Great Persecution came to an end in 311, when Emperor Galerius issued the Edict of Toleration. In 312, a new emperor, Constantine (272–337), claimed that he had received a vision before a decisive battle outside of Rome, a battle he needed to win in order to enter the city as the emperor newly proclaimed by his army. In that vision, said Constantine, he saw a cross—suffused with brilliant light—descend from the heavens as an otherworldly voice said, "In this sign [the sign of the cross] conquer." Thus, for the first time, the cross of Christ was wedded to violent military conquest. Constantine won the battle against his imperial rival Maxentius and was on his way to consolidating his power as emperor.

A few months later, In February 313, Constantine issued the Edict of Milan and granted freedom of worship to all religions, including Christians. But he did more than that. In short order, he returned all confiscated property to the Christian community, returned liturgical books[40] and books of Scripture,[41] and gave land and funding in Rome to build monumental churches—basilicas—that included St. John Lateran (the first monumental public church), St. Peter's on the Vatican Hill,

---

[40] The books used by leaders to guide the worship of the Christian assembly. The term "liturgy" is an Anglicized form of the Greek *leitourgia*, "the common work of the people"—a term used to describe the active participation of the worshiping assembly in its various ritual actions.

[41] The list of books in the Bible as known by Christians today was not completed until 393 at the Synod of Hippo. There the Christian bishops agreed to the list of twenty-seven books that constitute the New Testament, or the Christian Scriptures.

St. Paul Outside the Walls, St. Lawrence, and the Mausoleum of Santa Costanza. He transformed Sunday into a day of rest. Many Christians who survived the Great Persecution of Diocletian praised Constantine's benevolence and what appeared to be his patronage of the Christian community. But was he a Christian? Perhaps not. He refused baptism until he was on his deathbed, and he was not opposed to the religion of his father, which worshiped the sun god, or *Sol Invictus*, the "Unconquerable Sun." One then wonders if Constantine viewed Christians as one more powerful organization and sought the favor of their God as he did the Roman god of his father.

In 324, Constantine left Rome, never to return in residence again. He founded a new city—Constantinople, named after him—on a smaller settlement called Byzantium. This new city was located on the Bosporus, the channel of water where eastern Greece met Roman Asia. This move was intended to place the imperial bureaucracy closer to the east and the border where military incursions were increasing. Constantine's mother, Helena, exercised considerable influence over her son in terms of religion. He filled what he called the "new Rome" with magnificent buildings, including the Church of Holy Peace, *Hagia Eirene*—a church that commemorated one of Constantine's military victories. Note once more his conflation of religion with military power. In 325 he called for a council of bishops to gather outside of Constantinople in Nicaea. At this first council after his decree of toleration, Constantine called himself an apostle of Jesus Christ and frequently intervened in theological discussions. This is the moment when some Christian leaders became skeptical of his patronage—for who was he to judge a heated debate concerning theology, an army general with little knowledge of Christian faith and life? Constantine was well aware of the fact that Christians did not agree in their understanding of God—in their theology. There was ample diversity in worship and belief throughout the empire. As the one emperor ruling a vast territory now threatened with invasions, would it not be to his advantage to have a religion with a growing number of adherents marked by uniformity rather than diversity in viewpoint? And would it not be to his advantage to claim some measure of control over this expanding movement?

The emperor's departure from Rome produced a political vacuum. The metropolis retained its aura as the Eternal City—after all, it had been the capital of the "civilized world" for close to a thousand years. The Senate, its members frequently drawn from elite Roman families, continued to meet, though the Senate's actual authority had begun to diminish with the stripping away of its legislative powers. The privileged families of the city saw themselves as preservers of Rome's ancient tradition as the *caput mundi*, the "head of the world," though they were defending a memory rather than a living reality. At the same time, the population was in decline, trade was diminishing, and the city was at considerable distance from invasions north of the Alps; the army's generals preferred Milan to Rome as a staging ground for defense of the empire.

What remained was the bishop of Rome and the city's growing number of Christians. At first, there was considerable resistance to the expansion of Christian influence and Christian buildings in the city; Rome's senatorial families and public bureaucracy rigorously defended the ancient religion of the gods against this upstart group. All that began to change, however, when the emperor Theodosius (347–95), with his co-emperors Gratian and Valentinian II, issued the decree *Cunctos populos* (To All the People) in February 380. This decree of less than 200 words would have the most significant influence in Western Christianity for the next 1,400 years—for Theodosius and his colleagues declared the Christian faith, as expressed at Nicaea, *the one legitimate religion of the empire.* Henceforth, there would be no funding for the ancient religion of Rome—or any polytheist religion, for that matter. In quick order, Theodosius expelled bishops who disagreed with him and ordered punishment for any church leader who departed from his particular view of Christian faith and life.

What had begun with Constantine's patronage of a *movement* committed to the reign of God ended with its transformation into an *established imperial institution* in which the reign of God was easily conflated with the reign of the emperor. Of course, the church continued to welcome people into its life through baptism. Christians gathered to celebrate the Lord's Supper, the Eucharist. Bishops—regional supervisors—were elected by the people, and priests and deacons served in neighborhoods—though clergy were exempted from taxes and compulsory public service, and bishops could now serve as judges in court cases. The central practices of the Christian community continued but now as the privileged religion of the state. Was one being baptized into the kingdom of God *and* the kingdom of the emperor? For some, it was difficult to discern the difference. Within seventy years, the once-persecuted movement was transformed by imperial edict—a triumph, said the supporters of imperial Christianity.

In his masterful history of Rome, Richard Krautheimer notes that the ancient religion of the gods was suppressed in 395, and members of Rome's elite and powerful families were forced to convert to the new imperial religion. He then suggests that "as Rome turned ever more Christian, *the Church turned Roman.*"[42] After all, the church had become rich, "its economic interests wed to those of the great land-holding families. . . . And the hierarchy of the Church [had] been penetrated by educated patricians and by intellectuals linked to their circles."[43] Within fifty years of the suppression of Rome's ancient religion and the forced conversion of her many and powerful families, "a new Rome, Christian and classical, the

---

[42] Richard Krautheimer, *Rome: Profile of a City, 312–1308* (Princeton: Princeton University Press, 2000), 39; emphasis mine.

[43] Krautheimer, *Rome*, 39.

capital of the pope as spiritual leader of the West took the place of ancient Rome."[44] It was Pope Leo I who said, "Rome has become the Head of the World through the Holy See of Saint Peter."[45]

One sees this transformation of the Christian movement nowhere more clearly than in the image of Christ portrayed in the Roman church of Santa Pudenziana. No longer does he appear as a shepherd, healer, or itinerant teacher—images found frequently in the catacombs and house churches. In the apse of Santa Pudenziana, he is seated on a purple cushion, the chair itself a throne.[46] He is dressed in a rich Roman garment, a golden halo surrounding his head. Above his regnant figure, one sees a gem-encrusted cross, located on a hill. The apostles are dressed in togas of the upper class, with Peter and Paul flanking the figure of Jesus. They are positioned as the cofounders of a Christian Rome, these two martyrs replacing the mythological founders, Romulus and Remus. The apostles raise their hands toward Christ in a manner reminiscent of the gestures prescribed for those who entered into the presence of the emperor.[47] Christ holds a scroll on which is written *Dominus*

---

[44] Krautheimer, *Rome*, 46.

[45] As quoted in Krautheimer, 46. The term "see," as in "Holy See," is derived from the Latin word *sedes*, "seat" or "chair." In ancient use, the chair (or see, or *sedes*) designated a person of civil or religious authority. Thus, when Leo spoke of the Holy See of Peter, he was describing the actual chair from which the bishop of Rome would preach or teach as well as the authority of the office of the bishop. The bishop of Rome was thought to be in the line of spiritual succession stemming from Peter, who had been martyred next to the city's Vatican Hill. The term "pope," derived from the Greek and Latin for "papa," was applied to bishops and senior clergy for centuries. Only in the eleventh century was the term reserved in the Latin West for the bishop of Rome.

[46] Due to the incredible expense of creating purple dye, the color was at first reserved for senators and victorious generals or admirals, but by the fourth century, it became reserved solely for members of the imperial family.

[47] For an alternative view, see Thomas F. Mathews, SJ, *The Clash of Gods: A Reinterpretation of Early Christian Art* (Princeton: Princeton University Press,

Conservator Ecclesiae Pudentianae—"The Lord preserves the church of Pudentiana."

One wonders though: Why would the inscription announce Christ's preservation of a church? What needed preserving? Art historians date the mosaic's creation to the years between 410 and 417, immediately after the Sack of Rome in August 410 by Visigothic troops led by Alaric, their warlord. To say the least, the plundering of the Eternal City by "barbarians"[48] was viewed in Rome and throughout the empire as an unthinkable and shocking event. Perhaps, then, the inscription in Santa Pudenziana communicated gratitude for the preservation of the building from looting, burning, or destruction as Alaric's marauding warriors spent three days rampaging through the city. Yet the plunder of Rome heralded something more ominous: the weakened state of the empire in the West. With the weight of governmental and military strength in the East, the Visigoths found it relatively easy to march through the peninsula and assault the ancient capital. Only a few years later, the Vandals gained control of Roman colonies in North Africa. In 476, the Germanic warlord Odoacer unseated the young emperor, Romulus Augustus, and then gained increasing control over the Italian peninsula. Within four years of the deposition of Romulus, Benedict was born in Nursia, modern-day Norcia, a town in the Apennine Mountains of central Italy north of Rome. In 489, Theodoric the Ostrogoth invaded Italy and eventually murdered Odoacer. To say the least, Benedict was born into a chaotic and violent world.

1993), 92–114, in which Mathews claims the apse mosaic was less an expression of Roman imperialization and more a sign of episcopal authority—an authority, nonetheless, of one who held civic status and honors.

[48] The term "barbarian" derives from Latin *barbatus*: "ragged," "bearded," or "savage." "Civilized males" (i.e., Roman males), so the Romans thought, were clean-shaven or sported carefully clipped beards, whereas "uncivilized" males wore ragged, unclipped beards.

Benedict in Rome

The one source of Benedict's life is the biography written by Gregory, bishop of Rome, in 593, some fifty years after Benedict's death. It might be better to call Gregory's narrative a work of *hagiography*, a kind of writing intended to exalt the virtues of the central figure in order to inspire those who read it. Gregory's life of Benedict is found in book 2 of his *Dialogues*, a collection of stories about holy men and women who lived in Italy.[49] In 590, Gregory, a monastic priest, reluctantly accepted election as bishop and immediately faced considerable challenges. In 589, the Tiber flooded and ruined many of the fields that produced the supply of grain and corn needed to feed the city; growing hunger and starvation emerged among the population. Desperate to support the poor and hungry, Gregory called upon monastic communities in 590 to take charge of the *diaconiae*, the social assistance centers he established throughout the city. In the same year, Frankish and Burgundian armies invaded the Italian peninsula and threatened further pillaging. The bubonic plague, with its origins in the East, entered the city and region and began its deathly work.[50] Indeed, Gregory's predecessor, Pelagius II, succumbed to the disease. Wealthy senatorial families fled before the plague, leaving the administration of the city in the hands of Gregory. Elected as a spiritual leader, the new bishop was forced to supervise payments to public workers and manage a struggling program of social assistance, in effect transforming the

---

[49] For the critical editions, see Grégoire le Grand, *Dialogues: Tome II*, ed. Adalbert de Vogüé, OSB; trans. Paul Antin, OSB; Sources Chrétiennes 260 (Paris: Éditions du CERF, 1979); Terrence Kardong, OSB, *The Life of St. Benedict by Gregory the Great: Translation and Commentary* (Collegeville, MN: Liturgical Press, 2009). Quotations are taken from the Vogüé edition.

[50] This was the Plague of Justinian, an early form of the bubonic plague named after the Roman emperor in Constantinople. At its fiercest, the plague lasted from 541–49, with resurgences until the eighth century. Medical historians suggest that 25 to 100 million people perished because of the infection.

pope into an economic, social, and political leader who needed to address the challenges left unattended by those who had fled. Keep in mind that the imperial bureaucracy had moved to Constantinople in the early fourth century. Given the incredible turbulence of the time, Gregory's *Dialogues* was intended to inspire the Christian population of Italy with the lives of heroic and holy men and women—what Gregory believed were palpable signs of God's presence in the midst of social chaos.

Of Benedict in Rome, Gregory writes:

> Born of free parents in the region of Nursia, he was sent to Rome for a liberal education. But when he saw that some of his classmates were plunging into vice, he withdrew his foot that he had just placed on the threshold of the world. He was afraid that worldly knowledge might cause him to fall into the depth of hell. So, abandoning his literary studies, and leaving his family home and inheritance, he sought to please God alone. He went looking for a monastic habit so that he could lead a holy life. Thus, he left Rome learnedly ignorant and wisely uninstructed.[51]

Gregory suggests that Benedict left Rome because of the unseemly behavior of his peers and the "worldly" content of his studies. Some note that "he became disgusted with the paganism he saw" in Rome[52] and that "he was disgusted at the decadence he found in the city."[53] What might all that mean within the context of late fifth-century Christian Rome: withdrawing from classmates plunging into vice, fear of worldly knowledge, disgust at paganism or the city's decadence? Might we at least

---

[51] *Dialogues* II.1.

[52] Timothy Fry, OSB, "Introduction," in *The Rule of Saint Benedict in English*, ed. Timothy Fry, OSB (New York: Vintage Books, 1998), xxvii.

[53] *Dialogues* II.1.

suggest that there was more in the urban context that prompted Benedict to leave the city around the year 500 and enter the mountainous region to the east?

We know, for instance, the emperor Zeno, residing in Constantinople, commissioned the Ostrogothic warlord Theodoric to invade Italy in 489 in order to overthrow Odoacer and reunite the peninsula with the Roman Empire in the East. In this, Theodoric was successful, though military conflict ravaged the land. At the same time, Theodoric was an Arian, rather than a Catholic or Nicene Christian, in a city and region that held steadfastly to the creed created at the Council of Nicaea in 325.[54] Contemporary readers might find it hard to believe that mass demonstrations and public riots were prompted by differences in theology, yet such was the case in Rome during the second half of the fifth century. Felix III, bishop of Rome from 483 to 492, became alarmed by reports that Acasius, bishop of Constantinople, was sympathetic to a position that emphasized the divinity of Jesus Christ to the detriment of his humanity. If he was not *fully human*, thought Catholic Christians, was his birth, life, and death a charade? And if he was not *fully divine*, how would he be able to offer and effect the salvation of humankind? Felix's attempts to prod Acasius to clearly state the Nicene faith appeared to fail, and thus Felix abruptly excommunicated Acasius. Emperor Zeno attempted to reconcile the two bishops but failed. Thus, there emerged a strained relationship, both theological and political, between Rome and Constantinople. One rightly asks the question: Why should anyone care about a controversy between two bishops over what might appear to be an esoteric dimension of theology?

---

[54] Arian Christians held to a view espoused by Arius, a North African priest, who claimed that Jesus Christ was related to the one God but in an inferior position: he was less than God but greater than humanity. Nicene Christians argued that there was a fundamental equality shared by God the Father, God the Son (Jesus Christ), and God the Spirit.

The controversy did not cease during the time in which Benedict resided in Rome. In fact, it only intensified. In November 498, the archdeacon Symmachus was elected Rome's bishop at the church of St. John Lateran with considerable support from the people of Rome. Symmachus was committed to the Catholic or Nicene faith and was opposed to external pressure from Constantinople. On the same day, the archpriest Laurentius was elected bishop at the church of St. Mary Major with strong support from members of the nobility and Byzantine leaders who hoped Laurentius would effect reconciliation with the emperor and the bishop of Constantinople, a reconciliation needed in light of the Acacian controversy, and promote Byzantine presence in Rome and Italy. The election of two people with differing concerns for one position provoked demonstrations in the streets of Rome, demonstrations that turned violent. One can see, then, that class identity (people vs. nobility) and divergent views on foreign relations (welcoming or rejecting Byzantine presence) played significant roles in the chaos that ensued—a rivalry marked by deceitful propaganda promoted by both parties. Could Benedict not have been influenced, even "disgusted," by Christians fighting each other in the streets and circulating false and damning stories about the rival candidates for bishop?[55]

And what of decadence? Did Benedict discern a vast difference between the portrayal of Christ and his first followers in the gospels and what he encountered five hundred years later in Rome? We know that the Romanization of Christian faith and life was supported by powerful families who made Christianity "fashionable," who made it "acceptable" to themselves

---

[55] The case of the disputed election was taken to Theodoric. He ruled that whoever was elected first and with the largest number of votes would be the rightful bishop. Thus, Symmachus was declared the properly elected bishop of Rome, though this did not end the conflict between the two factions supporting the two men. See Jeffrey Richards, *The Popes and the Papacy in the Early Middle Ages, 476–752* (London: Routledge and Kegan Paul, 1979), 55–99.

and others.[56] Their patronage made possible the construction of monumental and lavishly decorated churches, churches no longer in the suburbs and at some distance from the Roman Forum, with its many temples dedicated to the gods, but now, strategically, at the heart of the city; the new imperial religion had displaced the ancient Roman religion at the ancient political and religious center of the West. "Old Rome and paganism were dead. . . . The Church was just as wealthy, papal gifts of silver vessels to churches looted by the Goths [in 410] were just as rich as before."[57]

At the same time, the imperialization of Christian faith and life could be seen in church leadership. Peter, a fisherman and disciple of Jesus, and Paul, a mobile tentmaker and early Christian missionary, were transformed into the twin patrons and "princes" of the new Rome, their images embossed in gold on glass souvenirs. The clergy now received privileges drawn from the Senate and imperial court: distinctive black slippers and white stockings, formerly worn only by senators; a fine white linen cloth or handkerchief, the *mappula* or *sudarium*, used only by members of the imperial court; and the *camalaucum*, a distinctive hat.[58] Let us note that Augustine of Hippo, Fulgentius of Ruspe, and Gregory of Rome—all members of monastic communities at one time—vigorously opposed the use of such elite insignia.

Many others warmly embraced such signs of privilege, thinking "it could only enhance the Church's authority if those who exercised this authority were invested with official badges

---

[56] Krautheimer, *Rome*, 27–28.

[57] Krautheimer, *Rome*, 46.

[58] Peter Llewellyn, *Rome in the Dark Ages* (New York: Praeger, 1971), 109–10; Theodor Klauser, *A Short History of the Western Liturgy*, trans. John Halliburton (London: Oxford University Press, 1969), 34; Hugh Wybrew, "Ceremonial," in *The Study of the Liturgy*, ed. Cheslyn Jones, Geoffrey Wainwright, and Edward Yarnold, SJ (New York: Oxford University Press, 1978), 432–37.

of rank and surrounded with *the splendor of the ceremonies of state.*"[59] Indeed, elements of imperial ceremony were increasingly employed by bishops: the chair for preaching and teaching became a throne; in keeping with the practice of emperors, bishops could order their portraits hung in churches; those who served them were admonished to cover their hands with cloth, kiss their feet, and kneel in their presence. These imperial privileges set bishops and senior clergy apart from the people they were called to serve and in effect produced a de facto caste system. In light of the utter simplicity Benedict embraced upon his departure from Rome, one wonders if he found the ostentation and enjoyment of such worldly privilege in the imperial church distressing, if not objectionable. One wonders if the peasant Jesus, crucified by Rome, had been forgotten in the wake of imperial faith.[60]

Concerning Benedict's view of education, Gregory wrote, "He was afraid that worldly knowledge might cause him to fall into the depth of hell."[61] What are we to make of this claim? In 535, some thirty years after Benedict's departure from Rome, the imperial counselor and soon-to-be monk Cassiodorus wrote to Pope Agapetus, urging him to establish a school in Rome where the Christian Scriptures and Christian writings could be studied: "Seeing that the [Roman] schools were swarming with students who had a great longing for secular studies . . . I was sad that the Divine Scriptures had no public teachers. . . . I urged Agapetus to collect subscriptions [donations] and establish Christian schools in the city."[62] The Roman

---

[59] Klauser, *Short History*, 35; see also A. G. Martimort, "Liturgical Signs," in *Principles of the Liturgy*, vol. 1 of *The Church at Prayer*, ed. A. G. Martimort, trans. Matthew O'Connell (Collegeville, MN: Liturgical Press, 1987), 188–91; emphasis mine.

[60] John Dominic Crossan, *Jesus: A Revolutionary Biography* (New York: HarperOne, 1994), 201.

[61] *Dialogues* II.1.

[62] As quoted in Llewellyn, *Rome*, 33.

bishop heeded this recommendation only in part and established a library—but no school—on the Caelian Hill, close to the ancestral home of Gregory the Great. Was Benedict interested more in the study of Scripture and early Christian writings? Did he find it remarkably odd that there was not a single school in the *Christian* capital of the West where he could take up such study?

And what of his classmates? Like them, Benedict came from a privileged family in which "masters"—younger and older males—were waited upon by "servants." Indeed, Gregory tells us at the beginning of his narrative that Benedict was served by a nurse or housekeeper, a servant or slave he would soon leave behind. Was it not only the lewd behavior of his affluent classmates but also the economic class structure they represented that he found distressing? Do we sense here an incipient discomfort with elite men who professed to be followers of the poor Christ, the servant Christ,[63] but in fact were "masters" adept at ordering others to serve them? Keep this in mind: though the historical Paul prohibited slavery among Christians[64] and some bishops preached against this Roman institution, Christian emperors did not abolish slavery. Did this practice—nothing less than the objectification and dehumanization of others—bother Benedict, a young man "who sought to please God alone"?[65]

What would anyone have encountered in Rome in the last decades of the fifth century? There were no longer Roman emperors; rather, a Germanic warlord styled himself a king. The Christian movement no longer experienced intolerance

---

[63] See the discussion of the kenotic hymn of Philippians 2:6-11 in chap. 1.

[64] See his letter to Philemon. John Dominic Crossan, "Paul and the Justice of Equality," in *God and Empire: Jesus Against Rome, Then and Now* (New York: HarperOne, 2007), 158–65. Crossan points out those writings in the New Testament that condone the cultural practice of slavery: Colossians 3:22–4:1; Ephesians 6:5-9; and Titus 2:9-10.

[65] *Dialogues* II.1.

or persecution as it had in the beginning (as documented in the New Testament). Instead, it had become the established religion of the imperial state and, as an established religion, had welcomed the wealth of emperors and powerful, elite families who had begun to insinuate themselves into positions of high church leadership. Monumental and richly decorated churches were built, subsidized by wealthy clergy and lay donors. At the same time, elite Christians fled the city when threatened with armed aggression or deadly plague, leaving behind their fellow Christians—the poor, slaves, and migrants—to fend for themselves. Economic status and political convictions animated riots, and dirty campaigns mounted against opposing leaders. Though Jesus and Paul had promoted a discipleship of equals, the clout of patriarchy and slavery had not subsided: young privileged men could easily order slaves or servants to do their bidding.

One wonders: Did Benedict, pious and new to urban life, encounter what appeared to be a *nominal* form of Christian life, nominal in the sense of *in name only*, nominal in the sense of giving lip service to that which was now considered a social necessity—self-identifying as Christian—in order to advance in society? Gregory writes that Benedict "withdrew his foot that he had just placed on the threshold of the world"—that is, the world of imperial Christian Rome. "Abandoning his literary studies, and leaving his family home and inheritance, he sought to please God alone."[66] That is, Benedict abandoned one path in life and entered another, with no idea where it would lead—except that ostentation, elite male privilege, social status, defamation of others, violence, and injustice would need to be sloughed off.

[66] *Dialogues* II.1.

3

Benedict's Refuge in Nature

Upon leaving Rome, Benedict fled to Sublacus, what Gregory called a lonely wilderness some forty-five miles to the east of the city.[1] Present-day Subiaco received its name from the Latin *Sublaqueum*, "Under the Lake," a reference to the damming of the Anio River (Italian *Aniene*) by Emperor Nero, who desired artificial lakes next to his luxurious summer villa.[2] Archeological evidence demonstrates that other villas were built along the river, but with the withering of the Western Empire under the invasions of the fifth century, they were left in ruins or destroyed by flooding. Among those

[1] "Benedictus . . . occulte fugiens, deserti loci secessum petiit cui Sublacus vocabulum est, qui ab Romana urbe quadraginta fere millibus distans, frigidas atque perspicuas emanat aquas" ("Benedict . . . secretly fled and went into a wilderness place called Sublacus, forty miles distant from the city of Rome, in which there was a spring with cool and clear flowing water"), Gregory, *Dialogues* II.1.4-5.

[2] Frontinus, *De Aquaeductu Urbis Romae*, ed. R. H. Rodgers (Cambridge: Cambridge University Press, 2004), 255. Rodgers suggests that Frontinus's reference is the only clear historical attestation of the Neronian villa at Subiaco. For the archeology of the villa, see Maria Tomei, "La villa di Nerone a Subiaco: scavi e ricerche," *Archeologia Laziale* 6 (1984): 250–59. For the Anio dams and images of the nineteenth-century painting of Benedict fishing at the river, see Norman A. F. Smith, "The Roman Dams of Subiaco," *Technology and Culture* 11.1 (January 1970): 58–68.

who lived in the mountains, at some remove from Rome, was Horace, the first-century Roman poet. In one of his letters, he spoke of the delights of living in nature; he praised the flowing spring, the woods and mossy rocks, the mild winters, the smell of sweet grass, the stillness of the forest, and the purity of the water as it murmured in the stream—that stream being the Digentia River that flows into the Anio before it reaches the Tiber.[3]

River

Some fifteen miles to the east/southeast of Subiaco, the Anio has its origin, its headwater, in a spring near the contemporary municipality of Filettino. It then flows westward through a gorge in the Simbruini Mountains, an extension of the larger Apennine Range. As a karst environment—one that is marked by underground water deposits—the Simbruini Mountains held and still hold a variety of water sources in caves and springs. Prized for its abundance, freshness, and clarity, the Anio was one of the major sources of water in the Subiaco Valley, the Roman Campagna to the west, and the ancient capital of the empire. The impressive force of the water surging through the ravine and into the Subiaco Valley was channeled into a system of aqueducts that supplied Rome with much of its water: the Anio Vetus (272–269 BCE), Aqua Marcia (144–140 BCE), Aqua Claudia (38–52 CE), and the Anio Novus (54 CE).[4] Horace wrote that not only humans but also a great variety of animals, reptiles, and birds found sustenance in the subalpine springs and rivers of the region.

[3] Quintus Horatius Flaccus, *The Epistles of Horace,* trans. David Ferry (New York: Farrar, Straus and Giroux, 2001), 47–50. The archeological remains of the villa in which Horace lived are close to contemporary Licenza in the Monti Lucretili, some twenty miles from Subiaco.

[4] David Deming, "The Aqueducts and Water Supply of Ancient Rome," *Ground Water* 58.1 (January/February 2020): 152–61.

As a student of the Bible, Benedict would have known well the following psalm: "You make springs gush forth in the valleys; / they flow between the hills, / giving drink to every wild animal. . . . By the streams the birds of the air have their habitation. . . . From your lofty abode you water the mountains; / the earth is satisfied with the fruit of your work."[5] His experience of life along the Anio was reflected in the psalm's praise of God's gift of water. Though he may have never studied the works of the Roman architect Vitruvius, Benedict would have grasped the truth in the civil engineer's claim that "all things depend upon the power of water"[6]—quite simply: no water, no life. No wonder early medieval Benedictine monasteries were dependent on and thus established close to water sources: Monte Cassino near the river Gari, San Vincenzo next to the river Volturno, Santa Maria by the river Farfa. For Benedict and many other creatures who inhabited the Subiaco Valley, the free and flowing water of the Anio was a veritable river of life.[7]

Food

Perhaps, in his departure from Rome, Benedict followed the Via Valeria until it branched into the Via Sublacensis, bringing him into the verdant and narrow valley bordered by steep hillsides, through which the Anio flows.[8] Above the river, writes Gregory, Benedict found refuge in a narrow cave set in

---

[5] Psalm 104:10-13.

[6] *The Ten Books on Architecture*, trans. Morris Hicky Morgan (New York: Dover, 1960), 226.

[7] See Genesis 2:10; Revelation 22:1.

[8] Gabriele Paolo Carosi, "Note di storia della communità monastica sublacenese: La stampa a Subiaco," in *I monasteri benedettini di Subiaco*, ed. Claudio Giumelli (Milan: Silvana Editoriale, 2002), 203. An older but still useful work by Thomas Ashby examines the ancient system of roads that emanated from Rome: *The Roman Campagna in Classical Times* (London: Ernest Benn, 1927).

the rocky face of Mount Taleo, an outcropping of travertine limestone dating to the Mesozoic era.[9] The cave or cleft rests some 970 feet above the river, the walk down to the water through a steep and wooded mountainside.

Benedict's cave was surrounded by a woodland of beech, evergreen holm oak, chestnut, hazel, and dense underbrush.[10] There he would have found alpine currant, artichoke, coriander, edible violet, fennel, parsley, red raspberry, rosemary, and thyme—all native to the region. Brown trout, lamprey, and crayfish swam in the Anio. Indeed, the medieval Monastery of St. Benedict, contiguous to the cave, holds a painting dated to 1428 that includes a young Benedict fishing in the river by one of the Neronian dams. In his life of the young hermit, Gregory speaks of the friendship between the young man and the monk Romanus, who from time to time would lower bread in a basket to the cave for Benedict's nourishment. One might gain the impression that Benedict was utterly dependent on Romanus for the intermittent gift of food, his seeming asceticism a sign of his holiness. Yet paleoecologists suggest that hillside and river offered plentiful sources of nourishment in nuts, berries, vegetables, flowers, greens, fish, and fresh water—all of which were readily available for human use.

One is mindful of Benedict's recommendation for the monastic diet set down in the Rule: two kinds of cooked food, bread, and fruit or fresh vegetables when available.[11] The one prohibition—of meat from four-footed animals—did not prevent the consumption of fish. Indeed, as Benedict's monastic

[9] Maurizio D'Orefice et al., "Un territorio da (ri)scoprire: L'alta Valle del fiume Aniene," *Bollettino della Societa Geologica Italiana* 102 (January 2014): 101–18.

[10] "Flora," *Parco Naturale Regionale Monti Simbruini*, accessed on June 15, 2021, at http://www.parks.it/parco.monti.simbruini/par.php.

[11] RB 39.3-4. All quotations from the Rule in this book are from *RB 1980: The Rule of St. Benedict in Latin and English with Notes*, ed. Timothy Fry, OSB (Collegeville, MN: Liturgical Press, 1981).

communities were established in the Subiaco Valley, they built fisheries along the river. Perhaps Gregory was unaware of or simply not interested in a memory known to Benedict's disciples: his fishing in the Anio, an implicit approval of their engagement with the considerable piscatory gifts of the river.

In his study of Roman aqueducts, the imperial water commissioner Frontinus noted the construction of a Neronian villa on the banks of the Anio. Such construction was prompted by the vicissitudes of living in Rome. The city was an unpleasant place during the summer months. The heat and humidity were oppressive and enervating. The smell of human and animal waste, slaughterhouses, tanning works, and acrid smoke from thousands of domestic fires—amplified by high heat and held in the air by high humidity along with the many insects attracted to the smell of food waste and excrement—was ever present. The vicissitudes of urban life during a third of the year pushed wealthy elites to build homes in the subalpine reaches of the surrounding mountains, homes set within a more amenable climate. Paleoclimatologists suggest that during the late fifth and early sixth centuries, central Italy experienced relatively mild weather prior to the cooling effects of the Late Antique Little Ice Age.[12] Indeed, temperatures in the Subiaco

---

[12] Drawing on tree rings, ice cores, and lake varves, as well as historical documents, paleoclimatologists have been able to reconstruct climate changes throughout Europe, and central Italy in particular, during the early medieval period. Here the claim is made that Benedict lived just prior to a sharp change in climate due to the emergence of the Little Ice Age, a cooling of temperature with corresponding changes in agriculture. See Scott A. Mensing et al., "Historical Ecology Reveals Landscape Transformation Coincident with Cultural Development in Central Italy since the Roman Period," *Scientific Reports* 8.2138 (2018), published online February 1, 2018, at https://www.ncbi.nlm.nih.gov/pmc/articles/PMC5794987/; Michael McCormick et al., "Climate Change during and after the Roman Empire: Reconstructing the Past from Scientific and Historical Evidence," *Journal of Interdisciplinary History* 43.2 (August 2012): 191; Ulf Büntgen et al., "2500 Years of European Climate Variability and Human Susceptibility," *Science* 331 (February 2011): 578–82.

Valley would range from cool in the winter to warm in the summer, with low humidity in the summer and light to moderate rainfall in the winter. This more pleasant weather offered a climate agreeable to human habitation: the valley was no harsh and harmful *desertum* but, as Horace opined concerning this region of the Simbruini Mountains, a verdant habitat in which the gifts of nature, the creation, would come into greater prominence for the young man who had left behind the conflicts and liabilities of urban life.

Cave

It is good to remember that Gregory's life of Benedict was a work of hagiography: his intent was to strengthen the faith and life of Christians throughout Italy in the midst of economic, political, and social chaos. He did not intend to offer a historically accurate biography of the saint. As a work intended to inspire sixth-century Christians, Gregory's writing drew on the Bible, in particular a number of remarkable figures in the Hebrew Scriptures who served as models of heroic virtue. In this regard, Gregory did not hesitate to illuminate his life of Benedict with stories of the Hebrew prophet Elijah, drawing a parallel between the two. Consider the motif of journey and refuge: having triumphed over the priests of Baal—the Canaanite god worshiped by the Israelite monarch Jezebel—Elijah walked into the wilderness on a journey to the mountain of Horeb, a journey to escape the wrath of the murderous queen. In the wilderness, he found shelter in a cave.[13]

But this was not the only mention of a cave in the Scriptures. Fearing for his life, the young David, future king of Israel, fled from Saul and found safety in the cave of Adullam, meaning

[13] 1 Kings 19:9, 11-17.

"refuge."[14] Here the rock enclosure served as a hiding place from danger. Consider the inscription of Psalm 142, "A Maskil of David. When he was in the cave," and the psalm's petition: "I cry to you, O LORD; / I say, 'You are my refuge, / my portion in the land of the living.' "[15] In his warning to the people of Moab concerning impending destruction, the prophet Jeremiah exhorted them to "[l]eave the towns, and live on the rock. . . . Be like the dove that nests / on the sides of the mouth of a gorge."[16] In their departure from Sodom and Gomorrah as the cities were being destroyed for their failure to provide hospitality, Lot and his daughters stayed in a cave.[17] The cave appears as a resting place, a hiding place, and a protective enclosure. In the darkness of the earth, one could become invisible. In the cave, one could find protection from threatening forces.

The cave also serves as a final resting place, the enclosure in which the dead are entombed: "Abraham buried Sarah his wife in the cave of the field of Machpelah facing Mamre";[18] "Abraham breathed his last and . . . [h]is sons Isaac and Ishmael buried him in the cave of Machpelah";[19] "[Jacob] charged [his sons], saying to them, '. . . Bury me with my ancestors—in the cave in the field of Ephron the Hittite.' "[20] This ancient Israelite practice is also glimpsed in the New Testament: "Jesus . . . came to the tomb [of Lazarus]. It was a cave, and a stone was lying against it";[21] "Joseph . . . laid [the body of Jesus] in a tomb that had been hewn out of the rock."[22]

[14] 1 Samuel 22:1-20.

[15] Psalm 142:5.

[16] Jeremiah 48:28.

[17] Genesis 19:30.

[18] Genesis 23:19.

[19] Genesis 25:8-10.

[20] Genesis 49:29.

[21] John 11:38.

[22] Mark 15:46.

And yet, the cave served not only as a burial site but also as a place of birth. The Protoevangelium of James narrates the place of Jesus' birth in this manner: "Joseph found a cave and led Mary there and stationed his sons to watch her, while he went to a find a Hebrew midwife in Bethlehem."[23] In the second century, Justin Martyr wrote of the same birthplace: "Since Joseph could not find lodging in the village, he found refuge in a cave near the village; and while they were there Mary brought forth the Christ and placed him in a manger."[24] The cave as place of birth has informed the iconography of the nativity in Eastern Christianity, its resemblance to the womb implied.

While the grotto above the Anio served as a physical place of rest for the young Benedict, we should not overlook its symbolic significance. As Gregory shaped his narrative, Benedict's departure from Rome was a *letting go* of those values and practices of the city and its established religion that he found disagreeable and at odds with his view of Christian faith and life: "he secretly fled and went into the wilderness."[25] It was nothing less than a dying or death to a former way of life. At the same time, his rocky hermitage was the place in earth's darkness where he was largely invisible to others: "In a narrow cave he continued three years unknown to all."[26] And yet something was gestating, something new was slowly *coming to life*. No wonder the medieval ritual of monastic profession would include the taking of a new name and the prostration of the monk or nun, covered by a funeral pall, as a symbolic dying to a former way of life and a rising into a new one.

---

[23] *The Infancy Gospels of James and Thomas*, 65–67.
[24] "Dialogue with Trypho," chap. 78.
[25] *Dialogues* II.1.4.
[26] *Dialogues* II.1.4.

Animal Skins

For three years Benedict lived in a mountain cleft. He had departed the social world of Rome but had not yet established monastic communities throughout the Subiaco Valley. He was betwixt and between his former life as a student and his soon-to-be life as a monastic leader. What Gregory implies is that Benedict divested himself of the privileges he had obtained in his former life: the wealth needed to support his education, his destiny as an educated person of influence and financial comfort, the probability of marriage and children, and the social benefits accorded males in an imperial Christian culture that had forgotten the egalitarian sensibilities of its predecessors. What did Gregory write? Benedict wished to be "worn out by labors for God rather than flattered by worldly praise."[27]

At some point during his time in the cave, shepherds in the Subiaco Valley caught sight of Benedict in the midst of the dense undergrowth that covered the steep hillside. At first sight, they thought he was a wild beast—*aliquam bestiam*—because he was clothed in animal skins.[28] This should not surprise. While Gregory might have included an accurate memory of Benedict's uncommon apparel, he was also aware of Elijah and John the Baptist, who wore similar attire in the wilderness.[29] Wearing a cloak or makeshift tunic of animal skin out of necessity would nonetheless associate the wearer with the fauna of one's region. At the same time, such attire expressed one's marginal social status; Benedict chose to remove the "soft

---

[27] *Dialogues* II.1.3.

[28] Earlier in the *Dialogues*, Gregory writes that Benedict encountered the monk Romanus, who *"sanctae conversationis habitum tradidit."* Translations differ: "He gave him the holy habit," or "He vested him with the habit of holy conversation." Confusion arises when the former translation is used (why would Benedict be seen in animal skins if Romanus had already given him a monastic habit?). I prefer the latter translation.

[29] See 2 Kings 1:8; Matthew 3:4.

robes"[30] worn by men of privilege in Roman society, including those bishops who dressed themselves with elegant and expensive imperial regalia as an expression of their "exalted" status.[31]

From an anthropological perspective, Benedict had entered into the "anti-structure" of a cave set in a remote valley, *anti-structure* referring to the rejection of the social structure and patterns of power in society—in Benedict's case, Roman urban life. Abandoning the pursuit of privilege and wealth—and the clothing that tangibly expressed such social status—the young hermit was on the threshold, or *limina*, of a new status. The cultural anthropologist Victor Turner notes that in a liminal passage from one status to another, "one [frequently] finds profuse symbolic reference to beasts, birds, and vegetation. Animal masks, bird plumage, grass fibers, garments of leaves swathe and enshroud the human neophyte."[32] Animal skins become more than the clothing for one's body: they express an altered status in one's life. No longer clothed in the "soft robes" and "worldly praise" of the dominant society, Benedict's change in life and purpose was expressed with a remarkable change in clothing, a change consistent with other ascetic figures: John the Baptist clothed in camel hair, Anthony of Egypt clothed in sheepskin,[33] and Martin of Tours dressed in the "mean" attire of sackcloth and goat's hair.[34] As Turner notes, "One dies in nature to be reborn from it."[35]

---

[30] Matthew 11:7-9.

[31] See chap. 2, pp. 49–50.

[32] Victor Turner, "Passages, Margins, and Poverty: Religious Symbols of Communitas," *Worship* 46.7 (August 1972): 411.

[33] Athanasius, *Life of Saint Anthony*, 47.

[34] Sulpitius Severus, *The Life of St. Martin of Tours*, 10, 14. Note well that when he resettled on the mountaintop next to Casinum (Monte Cassino), Benedict transformed a temple to Apollo into a chapel and dedicated it to Martin of Tours and then built a chapel in honor of John the Baptist.

[35] Turner, "Passages," 411.

If there is truth in Turner's claim, Benedict found himself living in a natural rather than a human-made refuge, in what came to be called "the swallow's nest,"[36] where he was surrounded by beasts, birds, and vegetation. With these gifts of creation, he found clothing and sustenance. This is to say that he was utterly dependent on the earth and other creatures for that which sustains life. To those who would prefer to see Benedict only as the great founder of Western monasticism, the teacher of wisdom in his Rule, or the exemplar of the fatherly abbot who represents Christ, any discussion of animality might seem uncalled for, if not mildly blasphemous. And yet, as a symbolic person—a person who holds a *surplus of meaning*, as does every human being—his connatural sympathies ought not to be overlooked or dismissed. After all, this was the man who spent considerable energy discussing the virtue of humility, a term derived from *humus*, the dark rich soil of the earth. To live into humility or *humus* suggested that the Christian and the monastic be rooted *in* the earth, *down* to earth, not puffed up, not "above" others, not arrogant.[37] Seeing Benedict *within* nature, rather than above it, allows one to see beasts, birds, and vegetation—God's creation—not as mere backdrop but as primary actors with the young hermit and soon-to-be abbot. Indeed, was this not Gregory's purpose in writing the *Dialogues*: to invite his Christian readers to see their lives and their land—though scarred by drought, war, and devastation—as healed and restored?

Raven

We know this: Benedict was an astute reader of the Bible, as evidenced by his many quotations from or allusions to Scripture

---

[36] A term attributed to Pius II (1458–64) in a visit to the cave of Benedict.

[37] RB 7.

in the Rule.[38] He would have known that on the fifth day of creation, God fashioned birds that "fly above the earth across the dome of the sky,"[39] and that after forty days of flooding, Noah sent forth a raven and then a dove, the latter bearing good news in the form of an olive branch.[40] In his teaching on God's providential care for all creatures—human and other than human, and regardless of their ability to be "useful"— Jesus asked his disciples to "[c]onsider the ravens: they neither sow nor reap, they have neither storehouse nor barn, and yet God feeds them."[41] That one finds frequent mention of birds throughout the Bible would have complemented Benedict's experience of the many birds in the Subiaco Valley: jays; sparrowhawks; magpies; green luis; dippers; green-backed, spotted, and white-backed woodpeckers; long-eared owls; yellow wagtails; and ravens.

His location within and openness to the wealth of nature can be discerned in one of Gregory's episodes: "At mealtime a raven used to come out of the nearby woods to receive food from his hand."[42] We find that friendship with animals, fish, and birds was not uncommon in the lives of early and medieval hermits and cenobites: Anthony of Egypt and a pig, Jerome and a lion, Helenus and a crocodile, Sylvester and a bull, Paul of Thebes and a raven. For Gregory, the figure of Elijah stood in the background as he wrote of Benedict and a raven sharing food: "The word of the Lord came to [Elijah],

---

[38] By 384, Jerome had completed his revision of the *Vetus Latina* gospels and translation of other biblical books. The majority of Benedict's quotations seem to have been drawn from Jerome's Vulgate translation, with a number of additional texts drawn from other sources, including the Rule of the Master. See Ansgar Kristensen, OSB, and Mark Sheridan, OSB, "Appendix 6: The Role and Interpretation of Scripture in the RB," in Fry, *RB 1980*, 469.

[39] Genesis 1:20.

[40] Genesis 8:6-12.

[41] Luke 12:24.

[42] *Dialogues* II.8.3.

saying, '. . . [H]ide yourself by the Wadi Cherith, which is east of the Jordan. You shall drink from the wadi, and I have commanded the ravens to feed you there.' So he went . . . and lived by the Wadi Cherith. . . . The ravens brought him bread and meat in the morning, and bread and meat in the evening; and he drank from the wadi."[43] Here we see providential care for one creature mediated by other creatures.

Yet Gregory's story concerns not only friendship between God's creatures but also Gregory's desire to promote Benedict's spiritual acuity. He notes that a priest, envious of Benedict's virtues, poisoned a loaf of bread and sent it to him as if it were a gift in honor of his virtue. Yet Benedict was aware of the malice kneaded into the dough; he recognized the deadly poison within and refused to eat it. When the raven arrived to join him for a meal, he spoke to the raven, asking it to take the poisoned bread in its beak, fly away, and leave it where no one could ever find it. Having dispatched the loaf, the raven returned and ate with the servant of God. Thus, set next to Benedict's spiritual powers—his remarkable ability to perceive the hidden and lethal nature of the bread—there is his friendship with this creature, who protected him and others from the threat of death.

Yet there is more. Adalbert de Vogüé, the distinguished scholar of Benedict and his Rule, suggests that the relationship between raven and human was a palpable sign of peace between God's creatures: "It is the return to paradise, the re-establishment of the harmony between creatures and man [*sic*]."[44] Rather than human domination over the earth and its many creatures, cooperation with creation, de Vogüé seems to suggest, is signaled in Benedict's friendship with the raven.

---

[43] 1 Kings 17:2-6.

[44] Gregory the Great, *The Life of St. Benedict*, commentary by Adalbert de Vogüé, trans. Hilary Costello and Eoin de Bhaldraithe (Petersham, MA: St. Bede's, 1993), 58–59.

"We believe that the divine presence is everywhere," wrote Benedict in the Rule.[45] And if that presence is truly ubiquitous, was it not to be honored in the most ordinary of creatures? In contrast to the objectification of bird or beast in the human gaze, it would seem that the friendship between these two creatures revealed the personality of each.

Spring of Water

Gregory speaks metaphorically of Benedict as a person composed of rich soil, well tilled and weeded.[46] Did he know that the Hebrew word for the first human—'*adam*—actually means "earth creature"? "[A] stream would rise from the earth, and water the whole face of the ground—then the LORD God formed [the '*adam*] from the dust of the ground, and breathed into his nostrils the breath of life."[47] Set next to a stream of life-giving water is the dusty earth creature. Within the rich *humus* of Benedict's life, continues Gregory, the seed of virtue brought forth fruit in such abundance that he became well-known and attracted disciples.

The growth of this first monastic household under Benedict's guidance led to the foundation of twelve small monasteries in the Subiaco Valley. "Three [of them] were situated on rocky heights so that it was very hard for the brothers to get down to the lake to fetch water, especially since the side of the hill was so steep. Among the brothers there was great fear."[48] Keep in mind the precipitous and rocky terrain that commences as the Subiaco Valley gives way to the gorge through which the Anio flows. Today the region is marked by paved roads and

---

[45] RB 19.1.
[46] *Dialogues* II.3.1.
[47] Genesis 2:6-7.
[48] *Dialogues* II.5.1.

well-used paths, but such was not the case in the sixth century. Benedict's disciples had to negotiate a perilous climb downward and then carry buckets filled with water as they ascended the steep mountainside to their monastic dwellings.

Gregory reports that a number of disciples approached Benedict, explained their predicament, and asked if they could move to locations near the Anio and the Neronian lakes, their closest source of water. Benedict invited them to return the next day. Then, during the night, he made the arduous ascent with Placidus, his young companion. Once arrived, he spent a long time in prayer, marked the site where he prayed with three stones, and then descended the mountainside. The next day, he told his disciples to look for the stones and dig into the soil beneath them. There they found water streaming forth "so plentifully, that even to this day, the water springs out and runs down from the top of that hill to the very bottom."[49] In Gregory's account of this wondrous sign, one can discern the figure of Moses, with his companion Aaron, striking the rock from which water flowed to assuage the thirst of the grumbling crowd (Exodus 17:1-7). But there is also this: As he slept on a stone, Jacob dreamed of a ladder reaching into the heavens. "[T]he LORD stood beside him and said, 'I am the LORD, the God of Abraham your father and the God of Isaac; the land on which you lie I will give to you and to your offspring.'"[50] When he woke from his sleep, Jacob erected the stone and named the place Bethel, the "house of God."

With Moses and Benedict, the water flowed abundantly. And in both stories, it was the intercession of each leader that prompted the Creator to provide needed water. While Gregory's intention may have been to underscore the spiritual gifts of Benedict—the efficacy of his prayer—one should not imagine that the servant of God was a mere wonder-worker (the ancient

---

[49] *Dialogues* II.5.3.
[50] Genesis 28:13.

world abounded with individuals who were thought to be thaumaturges). Rather, what one discerns here is trust in the providential care of God.

But is there more in Gregory's story of a stream flowing down a mountainside? After all, everyone who lived in a rural area of the peninsula sought a natural freshwater source in river, stream, lake, or spring. What Gregory does not mention is the ancient Latin name of the mountainous region in which Benedict found refuge: *Subimbribus*—today the Simbruini— meaning "under the rains." Indeed, its wealth of water was and is one of the most distinctive characteristics of the region. The winter snows in the higher mountains and mild spring and fall rains in the subalpine region, when combined with the soluble ground rock of limestone and dolomite, produced, over millennia, an extensive system of piedmont springs and streams. "Tight growths of woody and large herbaceous plants covered the well-irrigated margins of watercourses. So protected, the land absorbed precipitation and retained both its soils and the plant nutrients in them."[51] The Simbruini region was marked by waters that ran clear, cool, and stable. It was a water-saturated refuge for Benedict and his first disciples; indeed, water was a primary actor in this distinctive ecology. What Gregory does not mention is that, as pope, he gave water rights to the monastic communities founded by Benedict in the valley.[52]

Studies of monastic hydrology suggest that the establishment of early Benedictine monasteries began *first* with the search for a water source, a search that would determine where a monastic house would be built: "This was the result of a long

---

[51] Richard C. Hoffmann, "Economic Development and Aquatic Ecosystems in Medieval Europe," *The American Historical Review* 101.3 (June 1996): 633.

[52] *Chronicon Sublacense: Aa. 593–1369*, ed. Raffaello Morghen, trans. Arturo Carucci (Subiaco: Ediz. Monastero S. Scolastica, 1991), 187–88; *Il Regesto Sublacense dell'undecimo Secolo*, ed. Guido Levi and Leone Allodi (Roma: Reale Società Romana di Storia Patria, 1885), 252–53.

period of adaptation to the natural environment that could last twenty years"[53]—twenty years, perhaps, of searching, conceiving, and creating external channels and producing piping for water use internal to the monastic dwelling. What the wondrous sign of water flowing from three stones expressed was the challenge that all early monastic communities faced in Gregory's Italy: the need to harness and preserve water for daily use, and the need to build monastic houses from local stone.

Stone

In his life of the monastic reformer, Gregory speaks of a narrow cave and a towering cliff,[54] rough mountainsides and caverns,[55] bare rocky heights and a rocky summit,[56] towering peaks,[57] and jagged rocks.[58] While he was not a geologist, his description of the topography was accurate; the Subiaco Valley was a verdant area filled with diverse vegetation, trees, and streams, but all of this rested upon a platform of carbonate deposits[59] that were common throughout this part of the Simbruini region, a region resting on a bedrock ramp that dated

[53] J. M. López López, M. I. Pérez Millán, and A. B. González Avilés, "The Importance of Graphic Representation in Monastic Hydraulics," in *Water and Society III*, ed. C. A. Brebbia (Southampton: Wessex Institute of Technology Press, 2015), 378; Paolo Squatriti, *Water and Society in Early Medieval Italy, AD 400–1000* (Cambridge: Cambridge University Press, 2002), 19.

[54] *Dialogues* II.1

[55] *Dialogues* II.1.

[56] *Dialogues* II.5.

[57] *Dialogues* II.8.

[58] *Dialogues* II.28.

[59] Sedimentary rock formed by inorganic processes. See Simone Fabbi et al., "The 'Subiaco Stone' and the Early Studies on the Carbonate Successions of the Upper Aniene Valley," *Rendiconti Società Geologica Italiana* 44 (2018): 15–21.

from the Miocene epoch.[60] When Gregory wrote that Benedict marked a water spring with three stones, he was making reference to what modern geologists recognize as a massive layer and outcropping of limestone that supported the dense growth springing from the rich *humus* of the valley.

Of what were Benedict's small monasteries constructed? Gregory is silent on the matter other than to indicate that the first monastery, named in honor of St. Clement, served as Benedict's home. It was built upon the remains of the Neronian villa, a complex constructed with limestone, the carbonate sedimentary rock readily available in the region.[61] The value of this travertine rock is its capacity to bear heavy loads when compressed, stone upon stone upon stone. Covering the limestone foundation was a pattern of Roman brickwork—*opus reticulatum*—made of *tufa* (hardened volcanic mud), a tangible reminder that volcanic activity had left lava and ash in the Subiaco Valley.[62]

Here we see that the construction of the first monastic dwelling was made possible with local stone—stone drawn from a mountainside and from the effluence of long-dormant volcanic activity. It should not surprise us that when he discusses the variety of monks in his Rule, Benedict praises the cenobites, who "belong to a monastery,"[63] in contrast to gyrovagues, who

---

[60] The first geological epoch of the Neogene period, between 23 and 5.3 million years ago. See Simone Fabbi, "Geology of the Northern Simbruini Mountains," *Journal of Maps* 12.1 (2016): 441–52.

[61] Luchina Branciani, "Origine e sviluppo dell'eremitismo nella valle Sublacense," in *Le Valli dei Monaci*, ed. Letizia Pani Ermini (Spoleto: Centro Italiano di Studi sull'Alto Medioevo, 2012), 585–635; M. G. Fiore Cavaliere, *Sublaqueum—Subiaco: Tra Nerone a S. Benedetto* (Rome: Quattro D Editrice, 1994); Letizia Pani Ermini, "Subiaco all'epoca di S. Benedetto: Note di topografia," *Benedictina* 28 (1981): 69–80.

[62] Claudio Carrara et al., "Calcareous Tufa Deposits of the Aniene Valley between Vallepietra and Mandela-Vicovaro," *Italian Journal of Quaternary Sciences* 19 (2006): 19–44.

[63] RB 1.2.

are constantly on the move, free riders, drifters who take advantage of monastic hospitality but offer nothing to the community. "Let us pass them by," he writes, "and . . . proceed to draw up a plan for the *strong* kind, the cenobites."[64] We should not overlook his emphasis on the "strong kind" who belong to a monastery and thus practice the virtue of *stabilitas*. For what could be more durable than "strong" monks living in a stone coenobium? Benedict did not envision a mendicant life as did the Dominicans, Franciscans, and a variety of lay reform movements of the twelfth and thirteenth centuries. In a time of social chaos and disorientation, the virtue of stability was prized and lived within a stable and "strong" environment.

Benedict thus set forth a way of life anchored to one place as well as the natural environment of that one place, a way of life that would exist for the indefinite future. If one were wandering through a valley, forest, or mountain plain, perhaps the temporary shelter of a tree, grove, or cave would do. Permanence, however, demanded something else: something that would endure beyond the lives of those who found a home in the monastic enclosure. What, then, could be more permanent than stone placed on stone, a geological complement to a monk or nun vowed to a life of stability?

And what of the psalms they sang or recited together, psalms that promised steadfastness: "[I]n the day of trouble . . . [the Lord] will set me high on a rock"; "[The Lord] inclined to me and heard my cry . . . and set my feet upon a rock, making my steps secure"?[65] In a time of social chaos, would this name of God not gain the attention of those who prayed it: "a stronghold for the oppressed"?[66] While the temptation may be present to highlight the metaphorical dimension

---

[64] RB 1.13; emphasis mine.

[65] Psalms 27:5; 40:1-2.

[66] Psalm 9:9.

of such texts—as descriptions of one's spiritual or psychological state—their material dimension need not be set aside. Constructed of stone, the monastic enclosure provided rest as well as a protection, a stable environment as well as a space in which God, the "everlasting rock,"[67] was praised.

Benedict in Nature

Gregory wrote the *Dialogues* in a time of instability and its attendant chaos. His primary purpose was to strengthen and inspire the Christian people of Italy with the lives of women and men marked by heroic virtue. Writing as a monastic bishop, the devotion of one entire book to the life and wondrous signs of Benedict highlighted that for which many yearned: a sense of stability and the knowledge that God was continuing to act in the present as God had acted in the past—a past revealed in the prophets of the Hebrew and Christian Scriptures. From this perspective, Gregory invited his readers to recognize the topography of central Italy as another "holy land" not unlike the land in which God was present to Elijah, Elisha, Jeremiah, John the Baptist, and Jesus, through whom God performed wondrous signs.[68] Let us hold those two together—*holy* and *land*.

At the same time, Gregory included sufficient references concerning the valley to construct the natural environment in which the young Benedict received his calling to monastic life. Rather than let the land and water, the flora and stone simply disappear, we can see Benedict *within his natural environment* rather than above and beyond it and, in doing so, recognize the integral role this distinctive habitat played in his life as a

---

[67] Isaiah 26:4.

[68] Alison L. Perchuk, *Landscapes of St. Gregory: Hagiography, Architecture, and Environment in Medieval Central Italy* (publisher unknown, forthcoming).

hermit and monastic leader. Read carefully, Gregory's narrative reveals a consistent and harmonious interaction between the young ascetic and the distinctive ecology of the Subiaco Valley. In an essay published in 1974, the microbiologist and environmentalist René Dubos suggested that Benedict ought to be viewed as the great patron of care for the earth: "Benedict can be regarded as patron saint of those who believe that true conservation means not only protecting nature against human misbehavior but also developing human activities which favor a creative, harmonious relationship between man [*sic*] and nature."[69] Benedict lived in harmony with the creation and ensured that his disciples—marked by moderation in all things—would engage the soil and water with respect and welcome the gifts of nature into their worship, study, labor, and buildings.

But there is more. The one who abandoned the city followed the ancient stone road that led to the river filled with fresh water and fish—the water he drank and the fish he caught. Among the towering trees that surrounded his mountain refuge, the fertile *humus* brought forth the scent of smoky rosemary, anise-flavored fennel, tart currant, and citrus-flavored coriander. There was bread, too, lowered in a basket as if it were the manna come down from heaven. Having divested himself of the garments of privilege, he was clothed in animal skins and thought at first to be a wild beast, fully immersed in the animal life of the forest. No different from desert and forest hermits, he befriended a raven with whom he shared food—a friendship marked by the raven's removal of poisonous bread. Because they were dependent on water for life, his prayer enabled his disciples, who lived at a perilous remove from the Anio, to find a spring marked by stones, a spring that

---

[69] René Dubos, "Franciscan Conservation versus Benedictine Stewardship," in *Ecology and Religion in History*, ed. David and Eileen Spring (New York: Harper & Row, 1974), 130–31.

satisfied their need. We might focus, as does Gregory, on the wondrous power of Benedict's intercession on behalf of his brother monks, but we do well to note that it was the wondrous sign of water and its life-giving power that was the object of his prayer. When his reputation as a teacher of wisdom grew and others were drawn to join him in this reform of Christian faith and life, the limestone and volcanic ash of the region became the enclosure in which "the Rock of Israel"[70] was praised.

All this is to suggest that the genesis of Benedictine dependency on and care for creation—so different from the domination and degradation of empire—can be traced to the young hermit's life in a verdant wilderness, traced to the biblical texts he read that praised Christ as the agent of creation, the new creature, and the firstborn of all creation. Divested of social privilege and its ability to distract one from God and the ubiquitous divine presence, he was able to *see* this particular ecology and undertake a harmonious relationship with its many living gifts.

[70] 2 Samuel 23:3.

4

Praying the Seasons
of Life on God's Earth

In the modern global economy, time becomes a flow with no beginning and no end. The movement of goods and trading in stock take place every day, every hour of every day, and every day of the year. Wall Street may close at 4:00 in the afternoon, yet other markets are opening across the globe at that same time. Though federal holidays may offer a brief respite from work for many, labor continues unabated in other parts of the world. Such incessant commercial activity is made possible by the internet, global transportation systems, artificial lighting, and the millions of people who struggle with poverty—people compelled to work whenever work becomes available, at any hour, on any day. While the construction of buildings needs daylight much of the time, other forms of work continue with different shifts throughout the day and night. Human use of electrical lighting—a recent invention in human history—makes dependence on the rising and setting of the sun seem superfluous. Such was not the case in sixth-century Italy.

The Day

For the ancient Romans, and thus for Benedict and his monastic households, the day was divided into two periods:

from sunrise to sunset and from sunset to sunrise, with twelve hours marking each period. The first hour of the day, the *prima diei hora*, was 6:00 a.m., and the first hour of the night, the *vigilia prima noctis*, was 6:00 p.m.[1] The twelve hours of night were divided into four watches, or vigils, of three hours each. Thus, the first vigil of the night was counted from 6:00 p.m. to 9:00 p.m. Of course, in summer, the hour of daylight would be longer—around seventy-five minutes at the summer solstice[2]—and it would be shorter in winter—around forty-five minutes at the winter solstice.[3]

It is good to remember that ancient and early medieval people had no streetlights. One's life was easily endangered by venturing forth without companions or a bodyguard—muggers and gangs came out at nightfall. In the remote regions of Subiaco and Monte Cassino, the night was marked by ab-solute darkness, a darkness that enabled one to see, without distraction, the stars and the waning and waxing of the moon. At night, the Romans employed an individual oil lamp, a *lucerna*, or a cluster of them hung from a tall stand for illumi-nation, albeit dim illumination.[4] The night hours were given over to sleep.

One's sense of time was not measured by a watch on a wrist or a clock on a wall—what we may take for granted—but rather guided by the rising and setting of the sun, by *natural*

---

[1] The first hour, Prime, at 6:00 a.m.; the third hour, Terce, at 9:00 a.m.; the sixth hour, Sext, at 12:00 p.m.; the ninth hour, None, at 3:00 p.m. "It was the *third hour* when they crucified Jesus. . . . at the *ninth hour* Jesus cried out in a loud voice, 'Eloi, Eloi, lema sabachthani?' which is translated, 'My God, my God, why have you forsaken me?' He gave a loud cry and breathed his last" (Mark 15:25, 34, 37; translation mine).

[2] The longest period of daylight, between June 20 and 22.

[3] The shortest period of daylight, December 21 or 22.

[4] We know that candles were produced among the Romans, but due to the prevalence of olive oil throughout the Italian peninsula, particularly in the central region of Rome, Subiaco, and Monte Cassino as well as the south-ern region, oil lamps were cheaper and thus more widely used.

light. One awakened with first light and retired for the night with the last glimmer of daylight, earlier in the winter and later in the summer. Consequently, Benedict and his monastic households were drawn to this fiery star and its symbolism. Indeed, his Rule sets forth times for communal prayer in tune with the movement of the sun through the sky: Lauds at first light, Prime at 6:00 a.m., Terce at 9:00 a.m., Sext at noon, None at 3:00 p.m., and Vespers at 6:00 p.m. Compline was celebrated just prior to retirement for the night, and Vigils were kept in the third night vigil, possibly at 1:00 a.m. or 2:00 a.m.[5] "Seven times a day I praise you because your judgments are righteous," wrote the psalmist—the inspiration for Benedict's pattern of daily prayer.[6] Thus, the practice of singing the psalms, reading from Scripture, singing a hymn, and praying the Lord's Prayer was in concert with and yoked to the passage of natural light: its emergence, growth, zenith, diminishment, and passing from sight. "From the rising of the sun to its setting / the name of the LORD is to be praised."[7]

While imperial Rome worshiped the sun itself—consider the cult of the Unconquerable Sun with which Emperor Constantine was raised—Christians understood the sun, the moon, and the stars to be natural and beloved gifts created by the triune God: "In the beginning was the Word, and the Word was with God. . . . All things came into being through him, and without him not one thing came into being. What has come

---

[5] RB 8.1-2. Benedict did not create this pattern of daily prayer from fresh cloth. His horarium was influenced by the Rule of the Master and the practice of Roman monastic communities. See Nathan Mitchell, "The Liturgical Code in the Rule of Benedict," in *RB 1980: The Rule of St. Benedict in Latin and English with Notes*, ed. Timothy Fry, OSB (Collegeville, MN: Liturgical Press, 1981), 379–408. Let us also note Benedict's awareness of the changing patterns of light throughout the year—from winter to summer—and his flexibility in assigning times for communal prayer.

[6] Psalm 119:164, New American Bible.

[7] Psalm 113:3.

into being . . . was the light."[8] Indeed, the image of the sun and its radiance became a powerful metaphor of God's presence: "[T]he LORD God is a sun and shield."[9] As with humans in every age—early medieval or postmodern—Benedict recognized that the earth, its creatures, and their vitality were utterly dependent on the radiating energy of the sun. A common life guided by the arc of light through the sky would thus draw an ecclesial or monastic household into contemplation of the cosmos: of the developing patterns of light throughout the day, the rising and changing shape of the moon in the course of a month, and the One who "determines the number of the stars; / he gives to all of them their names."[10] Many early Christians faced the east, the place of the rising sun, as they worshiped, a physical orientation in prayer inspired by the words of the prophet Malachi: "[T]he sun of righteousness shall rise, with healing in its wings,"[11] an image of Christ whose final advent, so early and medieval Christians thought, would come from the east. And we know that, in time, monastic architecture itself was informed by the progression of sunlight throughout the day.[12] And yet there was no worship of the sun. Instead, its movement through the heavens offered Christians the opportunity to praise and pray to God: "To pray at the cardinal points of the sun is to say . . . that the God whose deeds the community tells and for whose mercy the

[8] John 1:1, 3, 4.

[9] Psalm 84:11.

[10] Psalm 147:4.

[11] Malachi 4:2.

[12] See Ana M. T. Martins and Jorge Carlos, "The Essence of Daylight in the Cistercian Monastic Church of S. Bento de Cástris, Évora, Portugal," *IOP Conference Series: Materials Science and Engineering* 245.5 (2017): 1–10; Naoki Seshimo, "Light and Proportion in Cistercian Monasteries," *The Architectural League of New York*, July 17, 2002, accessed on July 25, 2021, at https://archleague.org/article/light-and-proportion-in-the-cistercian-monasteries/; R. Kevin Seasoltz, OSB, *A Sense of the Sacred: Theological Foundations of Christian Architecture and Art* (New York: Continuum, 2005), 124–27.

community hopes created the sun and the moon, all the time-keepers, the great lights, indeed, all of the world itself."[13]

The Rule indicates that an Ambrosian hymn be sung at certain hours, a reference to the hymns composed by Ambrose, bishop of Milan from 374 to 397. In these lyrics, one finds the intermingling of nature's light with the light who is Christ. Ambrose praises the sun as herald and lightbearer "who scatters shade from day," the source of "luster shining bright," the "chariot," the rising dawn that runs across the heavens, and the "gracious light that dresses the day."[14] He speaks of the moon as nighttime light for wayfarers, the gifts of sleep and freedom from anxious toil offered by the darkness of night, and the deep gloom of nighttime that shutters up the day. The sun and its light also serve as metaphors for the Holy Trinity. Ambrose speaks of God as the *aeterne conditor*, the "Eternal Maker," who rules the night and day and gives to time its proper times. Christ is the light who shines on human senses, the light that "shakes sleep from the heart" so that the first human utterance upon waking will be a song addressed to the light of light. He is the true sun who gleams with an "everlasting glow" that suffuses the life of Christians. His Spirit is one who beams all-powerful grace into human senses.[15]

Of course, the metaphorical interpretation of God's power and presence was and is dependent on the careful observation of natural light—the light of the sun, the moon, and the stars—not simply as astronomical realities subject to scientific study but rather as manifestations of God's desire that all creatures

---

[13] Gordon Lathrop, *Holy Things: A Liturgical Theology* (Minneapolis: Fortress Press, 1998), 37.

[14] Brian P. Dunkle, SJ, *Enchantment and Creed in the Hymns of Ambrose of Milan* (Oxford: Oxford University Press, 2016), 221–24. Here we draw on four hymns of certain Ambrosian authorship: *Aeterne Rerum Conditor* ("Eternal Maker of All Things"), *Splendor Paternae Gloriae* ("Splendor of the Father's Glory"), *Iam Surgit Hora Tertia* ("At the Moment the Third Hour Rises"), and *Deus Creator Omnium* ("O God Creator of All Things").

[15] Dunkle, *Enchantment and Creed*, 221–24.

receive the life-sustaining energy that influences earth's climate and weather and the lives of all creatures, human and other than human. Perhaps, then, the triumph of modern science as the primary framework through which to view all created things in the heavens and on earth has eclipsed the earlier intuition that the day and the night come from the hand of a benevolent creator. For Christians of another age, the passage of the day and the night marked by sun and moon were received as living realities created and sustained by the Eternal Maker who gives to time its proper times. We do not witness among early and medieval Christians what many take for granted today: science deals with astronomy and weather, while religion focuses on the soul and morality. Rather, one encounters a holistic vision in which the movement of sunrise and sunset and the changing pattern of weather and climate are seen as integral to Christian faith and life.

The Week

We know that the week is a gift of the Jews to earth's inhabitants, a gift practiced and then recorded in the opening chapter of the first book of the Bible: "God called the light Day, and the darkness he called Night. And there was evening and there was morning, the first day."[16] In imperial Rome, the week was referred to as the *septimana*, "a seven," and its days were named after planetary deities (e.g., *dies Solis*, "day of the sun," or Sunday; *dies Lunae*, "day of the moon," or Monday; *dies Iovis*, "day of Jupiter," or Thursday). Such naming was intended to remind Romans of their obligation to honor the god who

---

[16] Genesis 1:5. This is not to suggest that other forms of marking days did not exist, only that the week of seven days eventually became a global phenomenon. Scholarly analysis suggests that the seven days of creation narrated in Genesis 1 is a possible borrowing from and reinterpretation of the Babylonian creation story, *Enuma Elish*.

"governed" each day. For the Jewish people at the time of Jesus, any association of days with Roman gods was thought to be idolatrous and repugnant. Consequently, the days were numbered rather than named (e.g., *yom rishon*, "the first day," Sunday; *yom sheni*, "the second day," Monday). "[O]n the first day of the week, at early dawn, they came to the tomb, taking the spices that they had prepared."[17]

Note that Christians and monastics kept the pattern of the Roman *septimana* but reinterpreted the seven days in a twofold manner. The keeping of the week invoked the work of God creating the heavens, the earth, and all creatures, the six days of creation yielding to the final creation: a day of rest (Friday sunset to Saturday sunset in Jewish practice at the time of Jesus). Here, then, was the opportunity each day to reflect on a different dimension of the creation: light and darkness on Sunday; the sky on Monday; land, seas, and vegetation on Tuesday; the sun and the moon on Wednesday; water creatures and birds on Thursday; creatures of the land, including human-kind, on Friday; and rest from creative labor on Saturday.[18] It was the keeping of the first day of creation, the day of light, Sunday, that inspired Christians to recognize the relationship between the *creation of the earth* and the *creation filled with the presence of the risen Christ*, who, they held, knew no boundaries of space and time. Thus, the author of John began his gospel with a clear allusion to Genesis 1 when he wrote, "In the beginning was the Word."[19] The gospels note that Jesus was raised on the first day of the week—a workday in the first century CE—and so, the evangelists imply, the spirit of the risen Christ is present in the very ordinary dimensions of life and in every day throughout the week (i.e., his presence is not sequestered to a particular "sacred" day or "sacred" place).

[17] Luke 24:1.
[18] Genesis 1:1–2:4a.
[19] John 1:1.

The early witnesses to Christian practice suggest that from Sunday, the day of resurrection, the week flowed forth, with each day an opportunity for the worshiping assembly to give thanks to the triune God for the creation and the presence of the risen Christ, the sun who gleams and suffuses the whole creation. Here we witness not a sharp separation of creation from salvation, with the latter focused solely on the human soul, but rather thanksgiving for the gift of creation held together in Christ, "the image of the invisible God, the firstborn of all creation."[20]

The Seasons

Living in central Italy, Benedict and his monastic households experienced the change in temperature, weather, and environment peculiar to this region that marked the natural seasons of the year as the earth tilted on its axis toward the sun. As the amount of daylight expanded, its zenith was (and still is) reached at the summer solstice, and then as daylight diminished, its denouement was marked by the solstice in December. The emergence of spring was and is marked at the vernal equinox with a corresponding change six months later at the autumnal equinox. With solstices and equinoxes, we encounter growth and diminishment, activity and repose. As we shall see, Benedict was attuned to the equinox.

In ways that modern urban inhabitants might find difficult to imagine, life in the agricultural economy of sixth-century Italy was lived in harmony with the changing seasons of the year: planting and sowing in the fields; the growing of crops, plants, herbs, and fruit trees dependent on sun, water, soil composition, and protection against invasive weeds, insects, and fauna; gathering and harvesting; and then storing what

[20] Colossians 1:15.

could be kept for the dormant season of the year. One's survival thus rested on the ability to gather nature's abundance, cultivate vegetables and fruits, and harvest grains. To state the obvious, there were no stores or markets in the isolated regions where monastic communities were established. Is this not one of the reasons why Benedict asks that each monastery be self-sustaining with its own "water, mill and garden" and various workshops?[21]

It should not be difficult, then, to recognize why the Christian and monastic keeping of feast days and seasons was (and is) intimately wed to the changing seasons of the earth: the lambing season at the vernal equinox (Easter), the wheat harvest in late spring (Pentecost), the greatest measure of light in June (the nativity of John the Baptist), the grape harvest in late summer (the assumption or "gathering" of the Mother of God into heaven), the olive harvest in late autumn (the preparation of sacramental oils), the chilling of air and land with the approach of winter, and the greatest measure of darkness in late December (the nativity of Jesus Christ). All these were turned, in the Christian imagination, toward marking the presence of the earth-loving Word of God, "through whom all things came into being."[22] The natural seasons and turning points of the year offered their own distinctive grace and challenge and, at the same time, were called upon to serve as witnesses to the birth, growth, public life, death, and resurrection of Jesus Christ.

In the context of discussing the Work of God, the daily prayer of the monastic community, Benedict notes two natural seasons: *summer*, from Easter (its date determined in part by the vernal equinox) until the beginning of November, and *winter*, from the beginning of November (with its chilling of land and air) until Easter.[23] He mentions the late-winter and

---

[21] RB 66.6.

[22] See John 1:3; references to the seasons are for the northern hemisphere.

[23] RB 8–10.

early-spring season of Lent,[24] the keeping of Easter[25] (at the lambing season), and Pentecost[26] (during the wheat harvest). One chapter of the Rule concerns the keeping of saints' days,[27] and another prescribes when the community should and should not sing the Alleluia—a transliteration of the Hebrew word meaning "praise the LORD."[28]

What we can discern in these chapters of the Rule is the significance of the day, the week, and the year attuned to the natural seasons of the land and the turning points of the equinoxes. But we can also discern their christological significance. That is, the land and the days and the seasons of the earth became the very matrix in which the life of Christ was marked and celebrated in parochial and monastic communities. Let us keep in mind that he was born in a rocky cave[29] and baptized in a river.[30] He proclaimed a year of rest for tillable land, laborers, and animals;[31] prayed in the morning and at night in deserted landscapes;[32] was familiar with fishing practices;[33] and spoke of sowing seed in different terrains.[34] He experienced

[24] RB 15.2. Benedict mentions Lent and the period between Easter and Pentecost. He makes no mention of Christmas, Epiphany, or the Triduum, though we can assume the keeping of the latter in his monasteries.

[25] RB 8.1.

[26] RB 15.1.

[27] RB 14. There is evidence in the sixth century of a feast for the nativity of John the Baptist, a feast for the dormition (assumption) of the Blessed Virgin Mary, and the commemoration of the martyrs. In the Rule, Benedict gives no names of saints to be honored in the monastic liturgy, but Gregory writes that upon Benedict's arrival at Monte Cassino, Benedict dedicated a pagan chapel to blessed Martin of Tours (beati Martini) and built a chapel in honor of St. John the Baptist (sancti Iohannis); *Dialogues* II.8.10.

[28] RB 15.

[29] Luke 2:1-7; see chap. 3, pp. 58–60.

[30] Luke 3:21-22.

[31] Luke 4:19; Jesus' proclamation of "the year of the Lord's favor" is an allusion to the Jubilee year prescribed in Leviticus 25:8-13, in which the Israelites were exhorted to let the land rest.

[32] Luke 4:42; 6:12; 9:28.

[33] Luke 5:1-11.

[34] Luke 8:4-8.

windstorms and perilous water;[35] was acquainted with foxes, birds, lambs, wolves, fish, eggs, scorpions, sheep, pigs, and calves;[36] interpreted annual weather patterns and signs in the heavens;[37] recognized the seasons of planting and gathering;[38] enjoyed the fruit of the vine harvested in late summer;[39] and kept the annual feast of his people's liberation at the vernal equinox.[40] That is, he was one with the earth.

At the same time, the New Testament praises him as the "one Lord . . . through whom are all things";[41] "the Word" through whom "[a]ll things came into being";[42] "the firstborn of all creation," in whom "all things . . . were created" and "hold together";[43] and the One who "sustains all things."[44] In one person, then, those who prayed throughout the feasts and seasons of the year could glimpse the *'adam*, the earth creature named Jesus and, *at the same time*, the second *'adam*[45] and agent of creation: not one without the other. In the paradox of Christian faith, one could discern the Creator in the creature. Thus, the celestial and terrestrial symbols circled around Christ as planets around the bright light of the sun. For Christians, he was the One who in his humility dislodged the emperor and his presumed domination over the creation.[46] Now liberated from imperial control and degradation, earth's many creatures could praise their Creator: "Let the heavens be glad, and let the earth rejoice; / let the sea roar, and all that fills it;

---

[35] Luke 8:22-25.

[36] Luke 9:58; 10:3; 11:11-12; 15:3-7; 15:11-24.

[37] Luke 12:54-55; 21:25-28.

[38] Luke 20:9-19.

[39] Luke 22:14-18.

[40] Luke 22:7.

[41] 1 Corinthians 8:6.

[42] John 1:1-3.

[43] Colossians 1:15-17.

[44] Hebrews 1:3.

[45] "Thus it is written, 'The first [human], Adam, became a living being'; the last Adam became a life-giving spirit" (1 Corinthians 15:45).

[46] See chap. 1, pp. 12–14.

/ let the field exult, and everything in it. / Then shall all the trees of the forest sing for joy / before the LORD."[47]

Psalms of Creation

Benedict saw the week as that period of time in which the entire psalter is prayed by the monastic community: "[T]he full complement of one hundred and fifty psalms is [to be] . . . carefully maintained every week, . . . [beginning] anew each Sunday."[48] At the heart, then, of the monastic and oblate communities that came to follow the Rule of Benedict, we see a spirituality shaped by the poetry of the psalms, a corpus of Hebrew verse that reveals a number of genres: psalms of confidence and others of heartrending abandonment; songs of royal enthronement and pleas for justice; lyrics sung by pilgrims and canticles used in worship; texts that narrate liberation from oppression and others that give thanks for the creation of land, water, and creatures.

It is these latter psalms, sung within an agricultural economy rooted in the land and its natural seasons, that ask for our attention. Why? A human-centered view claims that all things—soil, water, forests, creatures, and even air space— belong to humankind alone and that humans are free to do whatever they please with the earth—a sensibility we have witnessed in the Roman emperor's claim that he was the lord and master of land and seas; a sensibility that reemerged with imperial colonization throughout the globe in the sixteenth century; and a sensibility robustly embraced in the Industrial Revolution of the eighteenth century and its ongoing legacy of massive pollution, deforestation, and global warming. In

---

[47] Psalm 96:11-13a.
[48] RB 18.23.

this anthropocentric model, humankind commands from the top of an imagined pyramid that descends through levels of constructed value: colonized people; "higher" animals (e.g., dogs, monkeys); fish, birds, insects; flowers, trees, water, and forests; and, finally, inanimate minerals and rocks.[49] The lower one is located on this imaginary pyramid, the less one's intrinsic worth.[50]

The biblical psalms claim just the opposite: "O LORD my God, . . . [y]ou stretch out the heavens like a tent, / you set the beams of your chambers on the waters, / you make the clouds your chariot. . . . You set the earth on its foundations, / so that it shall never be shaken."[51] In the psalms, there is only one Creator; all the rest are creatures equal in their dependency on their Maker. In the cosmology imagined by the psalms, the heavens are glad, the earth rejoices, the seas roar, the fields exult, and the trees of the forest sing for joy at the coming of their Creator.[52] We do not discern a hierarchy of being in this global chorus of praise.

---

[49] This view is little different from the Great Chain of Being, a hierarchical structure of the cosmos with God ruling at the top and rocks resting at the bottom—a philosophical structure first promoted by Plato and Aristotle, taken up by Neoplatonists as the early Christian movement emerged, and wielding much influence in the Christian scholasticism of the high medieval theologians. In time, it was used by Europeans, trained in the *Scala Naturae*, to rank supposedly "higher" and "lower" beings when they encountered people different from themselves. The racist and misogynistic foundation of this ranking should not be overlooked.

[50] Here we see with increasing clarity the relationship between environmental degradation, racial injustice, and species extinction: those considered less valuable serve those who imagine they possess the greatest value; those humans perceived to be of less value are consigned to less-than-valuable (or even less-than-livable) living conditions; those species—flora or fauna—perceived to be valuable only for human usage become objectified and easily "used up" or extinguished.

[51] Psalm 104:1b, 2b-3, 5.

[52] See Psalm 96:11-12.

In a world where nations, corporations, and individuals can claim dominion over land and water and zealously guard their territory or seek to seize more, the psalm's assertion is an early example of *resistance poetics*: "O LORD my God, ... [y]ou set the earth on its foundations."[53] The psalms praise God as the molder and maker of the cosmos and all that dwell within it. That is, thanksgiving is first offered to God and God alone as *Creator*, as the One who brings into existence a diverse and marvelous creation in which each creature—from ladybug to majestic cedar, from gleaming gemstone to young child—is the object of God's favor and delight. In this regard, the earth is not created first for human use; it is created by God solely out of love for what God creates, each and every aspect of the creation marked by an intrinsic worth regardless of any function it might perform in an interdependent ecology. Keep in mind that Benedict and the raven were friends who shared food *before* the young hermit asked his avian companion to dispose of poisoned bread. Recognizing the worth or inherent dignity of the other preceded the "usefulness" of one to the other.

"[T]he LORD is a great God, / and a great King above all gods. / In [God's] hand are the depths of the earth / the heights of the mountains . . . [t]he sea . . . and the dry land, which [God's] hands have formed."[54] Perhaps for modern readers trained in the scientific theory of earth's creation and the evolution of species, the words of the psalm may be nothing more than fanciful mythic material lost to another age. Yet for the Christian who accepts the scientific consensus regarding earth's origin, there need be no disagreement between science and theology: the former examines *how* the earth came into existence and developed; the latter suggests *why* the earth came into existence and what might be one's purpose in this vast

---

[53] Psalm 104:1b, 5; emphasis mine.
[54] Psalm 95:3-5.

creation. For the psalmist who marveled at the depths of the earth and the height of the mountains, and for those who sang with thanksgiving for the creation, devotion to the Creator entailed serving as stewards of what God continually sustains on the earth. That is, humans were not called to be curators of a static creation but rather caretakers working with the Eternal Maker of a living, breathing, global organism.[55]

At the same time, a naive view of the creation overlooks its potential for damage and harm: "The voice of the LORD breaks the cedars . . . of Lebanon. . . . The voice of the LORD flashes forth flames of fire. / The voice of the LORD shakes the wilderness. . . . The voice of the LORD . . . strips the forest bare."[56] Did the psalmist imagine that the voice of God is so strong it can "[strip] the forest bare"? Perhaps. After all, ancient cultures ascribed powerful natural forces to the gods or God who they believed controlled them. What modern readers of the psalm might recognize in the metaphorical ascription of "flash[ing] forth flames of fire" is what different regions of the earth experience with increasing frequency: the potential for devastating wind, rain, or fire to defoliate orchards and forests and destroy homes and towns. We live in a world with ever-increasing forest fires caused by the warming of the earth and

---

[55] Let us note what at first appear to be two different accounts of human purpose in creation: "God blessed [humankind], and God said to them, 'Be fruitful and multiply, and fill the earth and *subdue* it; and have *dominion* over the fish of the sea and over the birds of the air and over every living thing that moves upon the earth'" (Genesis 1:28; emphasis mine); "The LORD God took the man ['*adam*] and put him in the garden of Eden to *till* it and *keep* it" (Genesis 2:15; emphasis mine). Dominion and subjugation, or stewardship and sustainable use? On the first chapters of Genesis as narrating the shift from a gathering to a farming society, see Michael S. Northcott, *Place, Ecology and the Sacred: The Moral Geography of Sustainable Communities* (London: Bloomsbury, 2015), 15–22; see also Phyllis Trible, "Ecology and the Bible: The Dilemma of Dominion," *Canon & Culture* (January 2012): 5–16; Lathrop, "Biblical Words, Contrary Words," in *Holy Things*, 38–45.

[56] Psalm 29:5, 7-9.

the scourge of arson. While the romanticization of the creation is an ever-present temptation, a realistic view recognizes that earth possesses a freedom to mutate and turn harmful. Throughout history, the vast majority of people have grasped that humankind cannot control earth's various forces—a realization that has now begun to dismantle the modern illusion of dominion over creation.

Living in a strong-group society that privileged common life and communal worship over individual freedoms and private prayer, Benedict directed the psalms be sung repeatedly, week after week, in order to shape the consciousness of a community turned to God rather than the isolated self. It is God, the Eternal Maker of creation, who is acknowledged in many of the psalms prayed throughout each day of the week. In this respect, the singing of the psalms and the Rule itself served and serve as a therapy directed toward the tendency, endemic in all human beings, to imagine the self alone as the center of life, the self as the one who reigns from the top of a constructed pyramid of creation with supposedly "lesser" beings below. No wonder Benedict wrote of the twelve steps of humility, of steps that would lead one *downward* into *humus*, into one's earthiness—into recognizing oneself as one among many creatures, animate and inanimate, in the creation.[57] "[The Lord] knows how we were made; / he remembers that we are dust."[58]

---

[57] Yes, Benedict does speak of reaching "the highest summit of humility" and the "ascending actions" needed in order to reach that summit (RB 7.5, 6), yet the steps he prescribes for the monastic and the Christian can also be interpreted as downward steps for those who previously enjoyed lives of considerable privilege, imagining themselves to be "masters" served by others in the social hierarchies of the early medieval world—the very thing of which the young Benedict divested himself once he entered the Subiaco Valley.

[58] Psalm 103:14.

If the psalms sung throughout the week portray God as the active creator of all things, they also praise God as *possessor* of what God creates: "The earth is the Lord's and all that is in it, / the world, and those who live in it; / for [the Lord] has founded it on the seas, / and established it on the rivers."[59] To worship this One is to recognize that no other entity can lay claim to an imagined "right" to possess the earth as his or her own private domain, as if he or she were the creator and thus possessor of the earth. It was the usurpation of this claim by the Roman emperor, who thought of himself as the lord and ruler of the world, that so distressed Jews and Christians. "The earth belongs to no other god, neither mythological or scientific,"[60] neither economic or political.

Should it surprise us, then, that Benedict speaks of private ownership—claiming anything for oneself—as an "evil practice [that] must be uprooted and removed [*amputandum*, or 'amputated'] from the monastery"?[61] He offers no support for this clear directive from the psalms,[62] yet one has to wonder if the psalms' insistence that "[t]he earth is the Lord's"[63] would lead him to recognize that human beings are not owners but rather tenants, laborers, who bear responsibility for the stewardship of what has been placed in their care.[64] In the ninth

---

[59] Psalm 24:1-2.

[60] Dianne Bergant, CSA, *The Earth Is the Lord's: The Bible, Ecology, and Worship* (Collegeville, MN: Liturgical Press, 1998), 5.

[61] RB 33.1.

[62] He paraphrases Acts 4:32, in which Luke claims the early Christian movement practiced dispossession of property and the communal sharing of goods according to need—Benedict's justification for writing that the members of the monastic community are to look to the abbot (or abbess) for their material needs.

[63] Psalm 24:1.

[64] The acclamation of God as creator and possessor of the earth appears repeatedly in the Psalter. Consider, for instance, Psalms 8:1-4; 15:1-2; 18:1-15; 19:1-6; 33:6-9; 89:8-12; 97:1-5; 115:15; 121:2; 124:8; 134:3; 146:5-6.

century, the Benedictine abbot and gardener Walafrid Strabo wrote of monastic *humus* at work in the earth:

> Whatever property one is given in the country, whether it is soft ground or a sandy beach where gravel still lies, or if it has brought about abundant fruits with its fertile moisture, whether set high on steep hills or open to the level plains below or rough with slopes and valleys, it does not refuse to bring forth native produce if only your care is not hindered by heavy lethargy. . . . You must not decline to *blacken your hands* calloused by a hard hoe, nor refuse to *spread dung* from full baskets on the dry dusk.[65]

According to Walafrid, labor in the field is intended to produce "abundant fruit" and "native produce." Through the agency of nature and human labor, God provides food and drink for creatures:

> You visit the earth and water it,
> > you greatly enrich it;
> the river of God is full of water;
> > you provide the people with grain,
> > for so you have prepared it.
> You water its furrows abundantly,
> > settling its ridges,
> softening it with showers,
> > and blessing its growth.[66]

Thus, in addition to proclaiming God the creator and possessor of the earth, the psalms give thanks to God as the *provider* of the earth's bounty. Consider, for instance, Psalm 104:

---

[65] Walafrid Strabo, "Hortulus: On the Cultivation of Gardens," introduction and translation by Ronald E. Pepin, in *A Benedictine Reader: 530–1530*, ed. Hugh Feiss, OSB; Ronald E. Pepin; and Maureen O'Brien (Collegeville, MN: Liturgical Press, 2019), 117; emphasis mine.

[66] Psalm 65:9-10.

O Lᴏʀᴅ my God, you are very great. . . .

You make springs gush forth in the valleys . . .,
giving drink to every wild animal. . . .
By the streams the birds of the air have their habitation;
    they sing among the branches. . . .

You cause the grass to grow for the cattle,
    and plants for people to use,
to bring forth food from the earth. . . .

These all look to you
    to give them their food in due season;
when you give to them, they gather it up. . . .
When you send forth your spirit, they are created;
    and you renew the face of the ground.[67]

Here there is not only praise—"O Lᴏʀᴅ my God, you are very great"—but also the recognition that God is the ongoing, active, and only creator of earth and its many natural treasures; no human creates and can claim to "own" the earth. Here the psalmist notes that all creatures—among them human beings—are dependent on God's offer of sustenance. There is an implied equality of dependence on God the provider among all creatures: wild animals, birds, laborers, cattle, and plants. The gifts of the earth are to be shared, not hoarded. To praise the provident Creator thus orients the community toward God and their dependence on God for sustenance and life. Yes, "[p]eople go out to their work / and to their labor until the evening,"[68] but there is no indication that they are free to use and abuse the land and water in any manner they choose. "The psalmist celebrates . . . God's exclusive and universal rule," yet the voice of praise yields to an ethic of amiable sharing in earth's natural treasures and expresses the notion that "one

[67] Psalm 104:1b, 10a, 11a, 12, 14, 27, 30.
[68] Psalm 104:23.

part of the creation cares for another . . . in an interconnected system of . . . ecological interdependence."[69]

A Spirit of Ecophilia?

In his directions for communal prayer, Benedict asks the community to pray in accord with the movement of the sun throughout the day and the rising of the moon and stars at night. He counts two seasons of prayer, attuned to the natural seasons of spring and winter. He notes Christian feasts and seasons rooted in the annual growth of flora and fauna, planting and harvesting. Poetry that praises God the Creator for earth and sky is encountered each week in the psalms. Taken together and read from an ecological perspective, the movements of the day, the week, and the year and the singing of Ambrosian hymns and the psalms conspire to cultivate what we might call an ecophilic spirit: a love for God's creation and the triune God. In addition, they offer an orientation to Jesus Christ, who, in the paradox of the New Testament, is called a creature of earth ("born of woman")[70] as well as earth's creator ("All things came into being through [the Word]").[71]

Such monastic praise for God's providential care of all creatures and natural forces stands in stark contrast to the wholesale killing of animals and humans in Roman arenas, the purposeful despoliation of water sources during armed conflict, the deforestation that produced deserts, and the poisoning of rivers and water tables with mineral extraction. Were early Benedictine monasteries aware of the legacy of Roman contamination and destruction of land and waterways? We have no idea. The earliest monastic *chronicae* tend to narrate the

[69] Bergant, *Earth Is the Lord's*, 33.
[70] Galatians 4:4.
[71] John 1:3.

lineage of abbots, the gift of land to monastic communities, and the privileges accorded them by the popes.

What we do know is that such communities were established at considerable distance from urban areas and the practices, infrequent or regular, that produced environmental degradation and made it seem "normal." While the monastic movement has often been characterized as a *fuga mundi*, a "flight from the world," let us be clear: the "world" that was being fled was not the earth but a social system marked by gross disparity between the many poor and the few rich, by normalized slavery, by patriarchal control, by the idolatry of imperial power, by the drive to seize more land with the use or threat of violent military force, and by the domination of land and water sources to support an economic system that benefited the very few. In their flight from *that* world and its imperial masters, monks and nuns entered the wilderness, frequently uninhabited spaces where they were called to settle and do so in harmony with that which was available in such natural settings.

Indeed, they had the opportunity to reverse the environmental degradation they had left behind by becoming "a respectful human presence, transforming nature into a space in which [humankind] cultivates a harmonious balance with nature."[72] Here we suggest that a "respectful human presence" capable of producing a "harmonious balance with nature" did not fall magically from the heavens but was nurtured in communal prayer. This was a prayer attuned to the natural cycle of the day, the remembrance of creation's gifts throughout the week, and the cold and warm seasons of the year; this was a prayer informed by ecophilic poetry that gave thanks to the Creator for the natural world and oriented the gathered

---

[72] Permanent Delegation of Italy to UNESCO, "The Cultural Landscape of the Benedictine Settlements in Medieval Italy," March 18, 2016, accessed on July 16, 2022, at https://whc.unesco.org/en/tentativelists/6107/.

community toward its common labor in the *hortus* of God: in the gardens, fields, orchards, and rivers that were found in and around stable centers of monastic life.

5

An Environmental Rule

Between his move to Monte Cassino in 529 and his death in 547, Benedict created the Rule.[1] Informed by his experience in Rome, Subiaco, and Monte Cassino, his study and reflection on the Bible, and his reading of extant monastic rules, Benedict produced what later generations have hailed as a classic of Western Christian spirituality. His prologue sets forth the purpose of the Rule: to be a compendium of wisdom offered by master to disciple, a path that leads to eternal life, a guide to living the Gospel, a school of the Lord's service.[2] One might easily conclude that the Rule is devoted to the spiritual dimension of Christian life and the practical aspects of that life in the monastery: for instance, monastic virtues, the practice of common prayer, spiritual reading, various forms of leadership, monastic vesture, and hospitality. Benedict thus offered guidance for the creation of a harmonious community committed to living a common life marked by holiness and mutual responsibility and striving to "translate into action . . . [the Lord's] holy teachings."[3]

As a *spiritual* classic, one then might be tempted to assume the Rule has little to say about a "harmonious relationship with

---

[1] The dates of his move and death are approximations.

[2] RB Prologue 1; 16; 21; 45.

[3] RB Prologue 35.

the natural milieu, sustainable development, and conservation of the environment."[4] Yet as we have seen, an *ecological* framework has helped us recognize Benedict's dependence on the natural habitat in which he first lived as well as the ways in which his guidance for communal prayer was shaped by the natural seasons and changes in the land. We ask: Is there more? What might the Rule reveal regarding the relationship between humans and their natural environment?

A Sense of Place

Benedict briefly mentions the spaces that constitute the monastic enclosure. An oratory is to be built and used for nothing other than the celebration of the Mass and the Divine Office.[5] The monks are to sleep in one place, what will come to be called a *dormitorium*.[6] The Rule speaks of the abbot's table and the food and drink served to the community from the monastic kitchen, a kitchen separate from the one reserved for guests of the monastery.[7] Guests are to be welcomed into their own quarters and dining room, separate from the monks.[8] A storeroom, bakery, and library are also mentioned in the Rule.[9] A newcomer to the monastic life, a novice, "should live in the novitiate, where the novices study, eat and sleep."[10]

Benedict's comments on spaces reflect his desire for the practices of the community to determine what is needed architecturally rather than for monastic practice to conform to

---

[4] Permanent Delegation of Italy to UNESCO, "The Cultural Landscape of the Benedictine Settlements in Medieval Italy," March 18, 2016, accessed on July 16, 2022, at https://whc.unesco.org/en/tentativelists/6107/.

[5] RB 11.13; 32.1.

[6] RB 22.3. From Latin *dormire*, "to sleep."

[7] RB 39; 40; 56.16.

[8] RB 53.21.

[9] RB 46.1; 48.15.

[10] RB 58.5.

other architectural models. In other words, the values and practices of the community determine its relationship to architectural space and the natural habitat. Though he spoke of spaces needed in the monastic community, Benedict gave no template for their size and arrangement. Gregory offers one exception when he narrates the founding of a monastery in Terracina on the coast, some thirty miles southwest of Monte Cassino. To the abbot, prior, and monks sent to establish this filial house of Monte Cassino on land donated by a "pious man," Gregory has Benedict say, "I will come and show you where you should build the oratory, the brothers' refectory, the place where you will welcome guests, and the other places needed for conventual life."[11] Gregory offers no description of that particular layout. What we discern in the list of spaces to be constructed is a *sense of place*. In contrast to wandering early Christian missionaries—Paul being chief among them— and the itinerant Dominicans and Franciscans of the thirteenth century, Benedict enshrined *no* mobility, *no* wandering about, a consciousness of one's natural habitat, of being rooted in a particular ecology where material existence matters.

The one given responsibility for care of the material life of the community is the cellarer: a monk who is "wise, mature in conduct, temperate, not an excessive eater, not proud, excitable, . . . or wasteful, but God-fearing, and like a father to the whole community."[12] The keeper of the community's goods, he is the one who has direct responsibility for "materiality." "Benedict gives a whole list of qualities the cellarer is to have, essentially the same as those for the abbot, and taken almost verbatim from Paul's list of qualities for bishops."[13] Would this surprise the cellarer: to be thought of as the abbot and bishop

---

[11] *Dialogues* II.22.1.

[12] RB 31.1-2.

[13] Judith Sutera, OSB, "The Rule of Benedict," in *Green Monasticism: A Buddhist-Catholic Response to an Environmental Calamity,* ed. Donald Mitchell and William Skudlarek, OSB (New York: Lantern Books, 2010), 79.

whose responsibility extends to every material aspect of the monastery, including its land?

Labor

Modern readers do well to remember that most monastic communities in the East and West were established in locations remote from urban life: deserts, mountains, islands, forests, and ravines.[14] The *fuga mundi*, the departure from corrupt and degrading values and practices in the "settled" world, led monastic founders to locate their monasteries in out-of-the-way places. This meant that building a monastic enclosure, gathering and cultivating food, securing a reliable water source, and obtaining clothing involved monastic labor. To state the obvious, there were no grocery, hardware, or department stores; physical labor was needed to supply the basic necessities of life. Benedict commends such labor as an antidote to idleness, "the enemy of the soul."[15] Yet his approval of such labor implies that it was necessary, a means not simply to curb indolence but also to secure and cultivate the very sources that would sustain life. There is to be no distress—no grumbling?—among the members of the monastery when it comes time to harvest crops, and even those who are sick or weak are given some form of labor appropriate to their condition.[16] "Beginning with Pentecost and continuing throughout

---

[14] Consider the Coptic monastery of St. Anthony in the eastern desert of Egypt, Mount Athos on the Chalkidiki Peninsula of Greece, the island of Skellig Michael off the western coast of Ireland, the forested monastery of Krastova Gora in Bulgaria, and the monastery of St. Benedict in the Subiacan ravine. Of course, there were and are exceptions to this practice. Monastic communities were present in Rome at the time of Benedict; indeed, when Monte Cassino was sacked by the Lombards, the monks fled to the city of Rome and lived there until the restoration of the abbey in 720.

[15] RB 48.1.

[16] RB 48.7, 24.

the summer," he writes, "the monks fast until midafternoon on Wednesday and Friday, *unless they are working in the fields or the summer heat is oppressive.*"[17] So worthy is physical work, says Benedict, that "[w]hen they live by the labor of their hands, as our fathers and the apostles did, then they are really monks."[18]

Thus we find monastic laborers gathering fruits and nuts, cultivating corn and wheat, and tending to vineyards, olive trees, and vegetable and herb gardens. During the early medieval period, "agriculture in lowland Italy consisted of the fundamental Mediterranean triad of [grain], wine, and oil, eked out with beans and fruits, which were mostly grown in small fenced gardens."[19] Indeed, the very act of taking up residence in a particular location, channeling a water source into the monastic enclosure, and establishing orchards, grainfields, and vineyards clearly engaged the monastic community with the local natural environment. But to what end?

In contrast to the overdevelopment of cities in the Roman Empire with the subsequent loss of urban greenbelts and groves, the depletion of farmland due to overuse, and the loss of forests due to aggressive clear-cutting, "monks had to be particularly careful to cultivate in such a way as to conserve fertility, for they did not have the option of moving on or buying alternative fields."[20] Concerning their care for tools, spaces, and land, Benedict offered a stringent exhortation: "Whoever fails to keep the things belonging to the monastery clean or treats them carelessly should be reproved. If he does not amend, let him be subjected to the discipline of the rule."[21]

---

[17] RB 41.2; emphasis mine.

[18] RB 48.8.

[19] Chris Wickham, *Early Medieval Italy: Central Power and Local Society 400–1000* (Ann Arbor: University of Michigan Press, 1989), 94.

[20] Michael S. Northcott, *Place, Ecology and the Sacred: The Moral Geography of Sustainable Communities* (London: Bloomsbury, 2015), 117.

[21] RB 32.4-5.

Do we not discern here a measure of care, of reverence for monastic holdings, including the gardens, fields, and orchards developed with monastic labor? After all, Benedict wrote, "We believe that the divine presence is everywhere"—*everywhere,* he taught.[22] And if such is the case, that this holy presence could not be compartmentalized as later generations were wont to do, would an ethic of care and conservation not attend their labor in what they knew to be God's creation?

Stability

For many North Americans, living in one home throughout their lives rarely occurs. The need to be mobile in order to find work or seek promotion in a career is frequently the norm. Thus, many will uproot themselves from one location and move at some distance from family and friends, a transition supported by what most take for granted: extensive road, train, and air systems; state patrols; emergency assistance; and aid centers for travelers.

At the same time, we live in a world that now witnesses the migration of close to 300 million people due to global warming and drought, armed conflict animated by drought and starvation, failed or dictatorial governments, and the desperate search for work.[23] For many migrants, safe and secure travel is *not* assured. Indeed, for many people hoping to escape war or starvation, mobility is endangered or hampered by poverty, gang or military harassment, and dangerous modes of transportation.

---

[22] RB 19.1.

[23] Marie McAuliffe and Anna Triandafyllidou, eds., *The World Migration Report 2022* (Geneva: United Nations International Organization for Migration, 2021), 1–4. This report takes into account the effects of the COVID-19 pandemic on migration patterns.

It was little different in sixth-century Italy. As Benedict moved to Monte Cassino in 529 and then began work on the creation of the Rule, the peninsula experienced the Gothic War (535–54), the Dust Veil Disaster (536–38), and the first Black Plague pandemic (541–49). Eager to recover the Italian peninsula and the western Roman provinces from Ostrogothic rule, the Byzantine emperor Justinian I ordered the invasion of Italy in 535; his military forces eventually met Totila, king of the Ostrogoths, in battle.[24] The length of this internecine conflict led to depopulation, economic instability, and the destruction of the road system, rendering travel exceedingly dangerous. In 536, volcanic eruptions produced a dust veil that encircled many regions of the globe.[25] The "veil" diminished the light of the sun, and without light, temperatures dropped, crops collapsed, cattle died, starvation increased, and armed conflict over remaining food stores wreaked havoc. With climate change comes conflict. Five years later, the first recorded incidence of bubonic plague entered the peninsula. In cultures that had no scientific means to determine the origin, transmission, and effective treatment of the disease, mortality rates increased rapidly. Though the plague is not mentioned in Gregory's life of Benedict nor in the Rule, it should come as no surprise that Benedict insists on the primacy of medical care for the poor and the sick who sought assistance at the monastery.

Together, these events, which took place as Benedict was composing the Rule, shed light on the Rule's first chapter, in which Benedict describes false and true monks. Imagine, then, a region in which military conflict has made travel dangerous, in which a change in climate has produced starvation, in which

---

[24] Gregory narrates Benedict's encounters with Totila in *Dialogues* II.14–15.

[25] Some scientists argue for a comet explosion on earth's surface as the cause of the dust veil. See Bo Gräslund and Neil Price, "Twilight of the Gods? The 'Dust Veil Event' of AD 536 in Critical Perspective," *Antiquity* 332 (2012): 428–43.

a deadly plague has prompted social isolation. No wonder Benedict viewed with contempt those "false" monks, called *gyrovagues*, who moved from region to region, "slaves to their own . . . gross appetites."[26] We might think of gyrovagues as free riders, those who seek the benefits of a religious organization but refuse to contribute to its life and health.[27]

Benedict praises cenobites, "those who belong to a monastery, where they serve under a rule and an abbot."[28] Thus, in a time of social chaos, he extols those who live in stable communities and promise stability, remaining in one monastery throughout their lives. While gyrovagues *drift*, cenobites are *rooted* in one place. And because of their stability, they remain rooted in and engaged with a particular landscape. While the thought of living in one home and preparing for the next three or four generations to live in that same home might seem fantastical to many people, Benedict imagined monks and nuns living in one location for many generations. He gazed on the distant future, not the immediate present. Consequently, his praise of *stabilitas* served at least three functions: it anchored men and women in their respective monastic communities; it created oases of safety and security for others in the midst of economic, political, and social chaos; and it drew monastics to engage the natural landscape in which they were settled.

If one were to survive and flourish for hundreds of years in one location, the monastic community would find itself dependent on the local environment: its water sources, agricultural capacity, and building materials. Without these, life would be impossible. Consequently, early medieval monastics could not afford to take for granted the hill, valley, or mountain where they lived. To be stable clearly meant to be stable in one

---

[26] RB 1.10-11.

[27] At the same time, we should note that in a time of social chaos, refugees or persons fleeing persecution would also be on the move.

[28] RB 1.2.

location and, thus, to know that location well. Rather than being a backdrop to monastic life, the natural environment became a significant actor in the development of the ethos of monastic life.

Thus, we see that Benedictine communities throughout early medieval Italy were founded close to rivers that flowed from springs or glaciers. A Subiacan *chronica* indicates that Benedict's monks built fisheries along the Anio.[29] Benedict established the monastery at Monte Cassino not far from the confluence of the Gari and Liri, in a region marked by an abundance of aquifers.[30] San Vincenzo was built next to the Volturno; the abbey of San Pietro al Monte gained water from the Toscio; the abbey of Santa Maria was erected close to the Farfa. What instruction did Benedict give concerning the one thing upon which all living creatures depend? The monastery must have a water source.[31] Indeed, water not only served as an agent in cleansing and cooking but was also used for liturgical ablutions and blessings.

The Rule asked that monasteries include gardens.[32] Herbs, plants, and flowers provided the infirmarian with the elements needed to produce natural medicines. Wine served as an antiseptic, honey as a dressing for wounds. Olive oil was used for the ritual anointing of the sick as well as for the lighting of lamps and human consumption. Grapes and grain were transformed into wine and bread—the central elements in the Mass—and also served as regular fare in the monastic diet prescribed by the Rule.[33] Here again we see Benedict's holistic

---

[29] Guido Levi and Leone Allodi, eds., *Il regesto sublacense del secolo XI* (Roma: Società Romana di Storia Patria, 1885): 252–53.

[30] Michele Saroli, Michele Lancia, and Marco Petitta, "The Geology and Hydrogeology of the Cassino Plain (Central Apennines, Italy): Redefining the Regional Groundwater Balance," *Hydrogeology Journal* 27 (2019): 1563–79.

[31] RB 66.6.

[32] RB 66.6.

[33] RB 39–40.

vision, in which the gifts of the earth serve material and spiritual needs, the two intertwined rather than separated into distinct compartments.

For monks and nuns in early medieval Italy, there were no building contractors, neighborhood stores, or state-run health-care facilities. It was by necessity that care for the natural environment grew: pollution of a water source, soil depletion through overuse, inattention to irrigation, and insect infestation spelled disaster in communities that depended on their natural habitat for water, food, and medicine. In other words, stability of place included the need to *know the place* and its capacities as well as to have an *ethic of care* for that very place. In contrast to imperial Rome and the poisoning of water sources through mining and sewage dumping,[34] monastic communities avoided such peril; their very life depended on attention to and careful stewardship of their natural habitat.

While he established twelve small monastic communities in the Subiaco Valley, we know that Benedict's first monastery was founded within the stone ruins of buildings once inhabited by Emperor Nero. Gregory writes that when Benedict arrived at Monte Cassino, he turned a temple dedicated to Apollo into a chapel dedicated to St. Martin and built a stone chapel in honor of St. John the Baptist.[35] Here we encounter the first instances of monastic repurposing: a local stone structure was transformed into an oratory, and stones were collected to extend the abbey beyond the existing Roman fortress that had been built atop the acropolis. We find a similar pattern of repurposing and building at Santa Maria di Farfa (ca. 700) and at San Vincenzo al Volturno (ca. 730); existing stone buildings—the ruins of a Roman villa, a fortified estate, and a funerary chapel—served as the foundation, albeit a modified

---

[34] See chap. 1, pp. 5–8.

[35] *Dialogues* II.8.10; 9.1. See Angelo Pantoni, OSB, *L'Acropoli di Montecassino e Il Primitivo Monastero di San Benedetto*, Miscellanea Cassinese 43 (Montecassino: Pubblicazioni Cassinesi, 1984), 81–99.

foundation, of the first monastic structures.[36] When additions were made, monastic buildings were constructed with *local* stone and built to serve the needs of the community.

What we see in the reconstruction of early medieval monastic buildings, in the archeological remains, and in extant structures from the period is a measure of *modesty* that would have been unknown in imperial Rome and among elite Christians who sponsored ornately decorated and monumental churches. Early monastic buildings did not dominate the landscape, shouting for attention. Rather, they blended into its topography. Concerning the earliest monastic construction of the Monastery of Santa Scolastica at Subiaco, we read, "The natural setting affected it in a sensible way, shaping its irregularity, its longitudinal direction, and its orientation toward a water course."[37] In their first articulation, Santa Scolastica, Monte Cassino, San Vincenzo, and Santa Maria shared in the conforming of architecture to the local landscape—an architecture marked not by the monumentality of the imperial Christian basilica or the later Romanesque monastic church but rather by a closeness to the land, a stone-bound stability without pretension.

Self-Sufficiency

It is not unusual to find produce in modern markets that has been shipped a considerable distance from other parts of the world: tomatoes from Mexico, pineapples from Hawai'i,

---

[36] For the Abbey of Santa Maria di Farfa, see Mary Stroll, *The Medieval Abbey of Farfa: Target of Papal and Imperial Ambitions* (Leiden: Brill, 1997), 17; for San Vincenzo, see Richard Hodges, *Light in the Dark Ages: The Rise and Fall of San Vincenzo al Volturno* (London and Ithaca: Duckworth Press/Cornell University Press, 1997), 62.

[37] Claudio Giumelli, "L'architettura dell'abbazia di Santa Scolastica," in *I monasteri benedettini di Subiaco*, ed. Claudio Giumelli (Milano: Silvana Editoriale, 2002), 14.

and tulips from the Netherlands can be found in a Minnesota grocery during a freezing cold winter—imports made possible by the invention of transcontinental airflight and trucking. Such a practice would not have surprised a wealthy Roman household of the first century; after all, they could purchase peppers from India, silk from China, and marble from Egypt. Indeed, the dining tables of rich elites were filled with imported delicacies unknown to the vast majority of the population. Yet by the sixth century, armed conflict and the disruption of trade routes made such imported opulence a distant memory.

It was in this context that Benedict asked for the placement of a water source, a mill, and gardens within the monastery.[38] While his instruction indicates what should be included in the monastic enclosure, it also signals a commitment to self-sufficiency. The community was dependent on what was available in its *local* natural habitat; there were to be no imports from distant lands. For instance, Paul the Deacon, in his *History of the Langobards*, notes that when they fled Monte Cassino as the Lombards attacked the monastic acropolis around 570, each monk took "a pound of bread and a measure of wine,"[39] suggesting that grainfields and vineyards were accessible to the monastic community. The Rule set forth a largely vegetarian diet, yet the archeological remains of the monastery at San Vincenzo al Volturno indicate the consumption of large quantities of pork, lamb, and goats.[40] The contract offered by the San Vincenzan monks to lay land renters prescribed an annual

---

[38] RB 66.6.

[39] Paul the Deacon, *History of the Langobards*, trans. William D. Foulke (Philadelphia: University of Pennsylvania, 1907), 163. The *Historia Langobardorum*, written between 787 and 796, may have been created at Monte Cassino. Perhaps Paul was simply repeating what he'd read in the Rule concerning the proper amount of bread and wine to be dispensed daily to each monk or nun. And yet, the region was known for vineyards and grainfields.

[40] Hodges, *Light in the Dark Ages*, 142–43.

modius of wheat and of barley.[41] The monastery of Santa Maria di Farfa was famous for the production of olive oil.[42] The monastic communities Benedict established along the Anio became proficient in fishing.[43] While the Rule suggests the restriction of monastic activity to the monastic enclosure, the clear evidence of vineyards, olive orchards, fisheries, grainfields, and animal pens suggests that much activity took place beyond the cloister.

Such self-sufficiency was undergirded by the insistence on common rather than private ownership of land, water, forests, and fields. It was the *common sharing* of the natural habitat that complemented an insistence on a *common stewardship* of earth's gifts. Private ownership could readily produce protectionism or envy of others, leading to conflict. Common ownership could nurture a sense of shared responsibility given by God.[44] In praying the Divine Office, the community chanted, "The earth is the Lord's and all that is in it, the world, and those who live in it."[45] And in the Divine Office, the community

[41] Chris Wickham, "The *Terra* of San Vincenzo al Volturno in the 8th and 12th Centuries: The Historical Framework," in *San Vincenzo al Volturno: The Archaeology, Art, and Territory of an Early Medieval Monastery*, ed. Richard Hodges and John Mitchell (Oxford: British Archaeological Reports, 1985), 237. The *modius* was an ancient Roman unit of dry measurement, roughly equivalent to two gallons.

[42] Gregory of Catino, *Il Regesto di Farfa* II.43, as quoted in Benjamin J. Graham, "Profile of a Plant: The Olive in Early Medieval Italy, 400–900 CE," PhD diss. (Ann Arbor: University of Michigan, 2014), 131.

[43] Levi and Allodi, *Il regesto sublacense*, 252–53.

[44] We note here a needed caveat: "As monks became unintentionally wealthy through their success in crafts and agriculture, they became increasingly religious professionals, scholars, and economic stewards. As they spent increasing amounts of time in prayer, study, and book-keeping, the monks ceased to participate in the holy work of manual labour that had been prescribed in the original rules of Columba and Benedict. . . . The decline of such labour among the monks led to the corruption of the monasteries." Northcott, *Place, Ecology and the Sacred*, 33.

[45] Psalm 24:1.

heard this reading: "The Lord God took the man and put him in the garden of Eden to till it and keep it."[46] The invocation of the primal human holds two functions: it conjures a metaphor of the monastic laborer and the monastic community as well as calls all members to the shared task of caring for the gardens and fields of the monastery.

This focus on self-sufficiency could also serve as a bridle on materialism, on the desire to gain more and more, a tendency discussed in Western and Eastern Christian rules: "[N]othing is so inconsistent with the life of any Christian as overindulgence."[47] Indeed, Benedict's guidance and that of other monastic rules underscored the need to avoid overconsumption and be content with what was available in one's particular location, to avoid the urge to request more than what was needed: "He will . . . issue to [the brothers] the various articles to be cared for and collected after use."[48] "[I]t is enough, we believe, to provide all tables with two kinds of cooked food. . . . Two kinds . . . should suffice. . . . A generous pound of bread is enough."[49] "The clothing distributed to the brothers should vary according to local conditions and climate, because more is needed in cold regions and less in warmer."[50] "For their needs, they are to look to the father of the monastery, and are not allowed anything which the abbot has not given or permitted."[51] These instructions suggest a clear teaching: "[I]n all matters *frugality* is the rule,"[52] yet it must be a frugality tempered by the awareness of human need and human weakness. When applied to the monastic landscape, overconsumption, and thus overuse, would deplete soil fertility, waste a

---

[46] Genesis 2:15.

[47] RB 39.8.

[48] RB 32.2.

[49] RB 39.1-4.

[50] RB 55.1.

[51] RB 33.5.

[52] RB 39.10; emphasis mine.

precious water supply, and diminish harvests that were to be shared with the poor, guests, and those who sought medical assistance from the monastic infirmary.

Simplicity

With Benedict's abhorrence of private ownership, a precept inspired by Luke's narrative in the Acts of the Apostles,[53] we recognize an economy informed by equitable sharing according to need rather than according to the hunger for more and more. Read carefully, the Rule frequently speaks of *moderatio*, having not too much and not too little. And that encouragement is determined by the needs of the sick, of laborers in hot weather, of boys given to the monastery for education or the monastic vocation. Benedict writes, "It is written: *Distribution was made to each one as he had need.*"[54] And that distribution is determined, in part, by attention to human weakness: if one is sick, one is given a bit of meat to eat;[55] if one is laboring in high heat, one is given a bit more food and drink.[56] In contrast to imperial Rome's thirst for more colonies to exploit and to the Gothic invaders' search for more land and more wealth gained through force, the Rule insisted on moderation and the distribution of goods according to need, especially the needs of the most vulnerable. Imagine that: a society in which care for the most vulnerable shaped its economic priorities.

Conservation rather than overconsumption flows from the Rule's emphasis on maintaining simplicity of life. Do we not hear Benedict and his monastic precursors saying, "Do not be

---

[53] "[N]o one claimed private ownership of any possessions, but everything they owned was held in common" (Acts 4:32).

[54] RB 34.1; emphasis in original. Here Benedict is quoting Acts 4:35.

[55] RB 36.9.

[56] RB 39.6; 40.5.

wasteful"? What prompted Benedict to flee Rome and enter the Subiacan ravine? Was it not, in part, the ostentatious display of wealth, of overconsumption, among elite Christians in a city with many people challenged by poverty and hunger? If one dimension of early monastic spirituality was simplicity of life, its ecological corollary was the need to conserve what was available in a particular location.

A Sacred Landscape

The great achievement of the Age of Enlightenment in the eighteenth century was to render the earth and its creatures objects of scientific examination and categorization. Such analysis in the nineteenth and twentieth centuries shed significant light on how the planet came into existence and how life evolved, how disease originates and can be treated, and how humans and other creatures live in a symbiotic relationship with their environments, dependent on the earth for their very existence. All this and more is cause for gratitude. Yet at the same time, the biblical conviction that the divine Creator is the ultimate source of earth's life was eclipsed under the weight of scientific "progress." Unable to find testable evidence for the existence of God, religious devotion to a divine Creator was treated as a "primitive" practice to be discarded by the "enlightened." The natural environment became an object not only to be analyzed but also to be used, frequently abused, and then thrown away for the sake of corporate profit.[57]

By way of contrast, the scriptural vision of the earth is marked by thanksgiving for the gift of the creation that flows

---

[57] "The earth, our home, is beginning to look more and more like an immense pile of filth. . . . These problems are closely linked to a *throwaway culture* which affects the excluded just as it quickly reduces things to rubbish" (Pope Francis, *Laudato Si'* 21; emphasis mine).

continually from God and by reverence for its diverse forms of life: from water to fish, from soil to plants. For monastics attuned to the Gospel of John, the creation was brought into existence by the Word of God enfleshed in Jesus of Nazareth: "All things came into being through [the Word], and without him not one thing came into being. What has come into being in him was life."[58] In his prayer addressed to the "eternal Creator of all material things," Autpert Ambrose, the eighth-century abbot of San Vincenzo al Volturno, echoed the Johannine hymn: "You are everywhere and yet you are not limited by anything, either materially or spiritually. You are wholly outside creatures . . . and yet wholly within each. You are wholly in all things."[59] Here, the earth and its creatures were not robbed of their numinous quality: the divine presence is "wholly within each," immanent, though never limited or captured by each.

When he discussed the duties of the cellarer, Benedict offered this instruction: "He will regard all utensils and goods of the monastery as sacred vessels of the altar, aware that nothing is to be neglected."[60] This was nothing less than a stunning exhortation. "Given the extreme reverence for the sacred vessels that has always been characteristic of Catholicism, this claim for the holiness of even the humblest cooking pot is not to be dismissed as a purple passage."[61] One wonders if Benedict were suggesting that the cellarer, the keeper of the monastery's

[58] John 1:3-4.

[59] *Chronicon Vulturnense del Monaco Giovanni*, ed. Vincenzo Frederici (Rome: Istituto Storico Italiano, 1925), 3.

[60] RB 31.10-11. "On that day there shall be inscribed on the bells of the horses, 'Holy to the Lord.' And the cooking pots in the house of the Lord shall be as holy as the bowls in front of the altar; and every cooking pot in Jerusalem and Judah shall be sacred to the Lord of hosts" (Zechariah 14:20-21).

[61] Terrence Kardong, OSB, *Benedict's Rule: A Translation and Commentary* (Collegeville, MN: Liturgical Press, 1996), 272.

material well-being, was to be seen as a *priest*, the one who cares for and distributes the "natural grace" of goods, those "goods" of the natural environment. What did he write? "[T]he divine presence is everywhere."[62]

Here we recognize again a holistic vision in which all things reveal the presence of God: "Benedict will tolerate *no dualism* between the sacred and the profane. All things are holy since they came from the hand of God, who looked on them and said: 'It is good' (Gen 1:4ff.)."[63] Might we then extend the notion of sacrality to the land itself, the preeminent source of the community's material life as well as its sacramental celebrations? And would such a claim serve as a needed criticism of the cultural propensity, pervasive among profiteers in ancient Rome and modern North America, to treat the land as nothing more than an object to be used up and discarded?

In his history of Europe's natural environment, Richard Hoffmann notes that monastic communities were cooperators with the land: "The prototype for western communal monasticism, the Rule of Benedict, obliged ascetics to work. That work was to be carried out in nature as a means of constructing the monastic environment itself, the cloister, the 'enclosed garden' (*hortus inclusus*). . . . The monks' labour made the walls within which they lived into a garden, and in making that garden they created a *paradisos*, not merely reminiscent of but replicating the enclosure of Genesis."[64] Perhaps this is why some have suggested that the monks and the monastic community laboring in the monastic garden, orchard, or field could be thought of as a "new Adam," tending and conserving God's earth.[65]

---

[62] RB 19.1.

[63] Kardong, *Benedict's Rule*, 271; emphasis mine.

[64] Richard C. Hoffmann, *An Environmental History of Medieval Europe* (Cambridge: Cambridge University Press, 2014), 103.

[65] Bernard McGinn speaks of Benedict as Adam; see McGinn, "St. Benedict as the Steward of Creation," *American Benedictine Review* 39.2 (1988): 161–76.

The Benedictine abbess and gardener Hildegard of Bingen grasped the sacral quality of the land: "God has adorned the universe with brilliance and beauty. He has filled it with the riches of creation."[66] Indeed, it is the greening power of God, what Hildegard called *viriditas*, that brings fecundity to gardens, fields, and orchards: "I am the breeze that nurtures all things green," says the Creator. "I encourage blossoms to flourish with ripening fruits. I am the rain coming from the dew that causes the grasses to laugh with the joy of life."[67] In this regard, Hildegard echoes Benedict's insistence on the holiness of all things. The abbot and abbess did not limit the presence of God to a person (e.g., a priest), a text (e.g., the Bible), or an action (e.g., the giving of the Mass). Their vision was expansive, recognizing the vibrant, active, and life-giving presence of God's Spirit in the most ordinary of things, the land and its produce a natural sacrament of grace.

Between 535 and 554, the Gothic War laid waste to the countryside of the Italian peninsula. Armed aggression and pillaging brought cruelty, material chaos, and moral disorder to the region. In such a context, one could well imagine the creation of a rule marked by isolationism, pessimism, and a spiritualization that denied the good of the created order. Indeed, a number of monastic rules from the period were marked by severe asceticism and an otherworldly gaze. Yet with Benedict, we encounter the primacy of love—for God, for other monastics, for strangers, for the poor—and an ethic of care for the garden, the river, and the land. To be sure, the Rule is not a

---

Mary Helms suggests that the figure of Adam served as the archetype for generations of early medieval monks who labored in the land; see Helms, "Sacred Landscape and the Early Medieval Cloister: Unity, Paradise, and the Cosmic Mountain," *Anthropos* 97 (2002): 437.

[66] Hildegard of Bingen, *Liber Vitae Meritorum* III.26, as quoted in Heinrich Schipperges, *The World of Hildegard of Bingen: Her Life, Times, and Visions*, trans. John Cumming (Collegeville, MN: Liturgical Press, 1998), 95.

[67] Matthew Fox, *Illuminations of Hildegard of Bingen* (Santa Fe: Bear & Co., 1985), 33.

treatise on environmental ethics, yet we find within it the beginning of an *ecophilic* spirit that would cultivate a form of life in harmony with the natural landscape. "Among the Benedictines whose order was established by St. Benedict in the sixth century . . . agricultural and forestry management practices were sophisticated and diverse. St. Benedict set an early example of sustainability: Benedictine communities had to pass on their lands in at least as fertile a state as when they found them."[68] However, such an "early example of sustainability" also stands as a potent criticism of any society that sanctions the "waste and pollution of God's creation and its lack of concern for those who come after."[69]

[68] Josep-Maria Mallarach, "Monastic Communities and Nature Conservation: Overview of Positive Trends and Best Practices in Europe and the Middle East," in *The Diversity of Sacred Lands in Europe*, ed. Josep-Maria Mallarach, Thymio Papayannis, and Rauno Väisänen (Gland, Switzerland: IUCN, 2012), 157.

[69] "Litany of Penitence," in *The Book of Common Prayer* (New York: Church Publishing, 1979), 268.

6

Monastic Ecological Values

On December 26, 1966, Lynn White, a historian of medieval technology at the University of California Los Angeles, gave a paper at the annual meeting of the American Association for the Advancement of Science in Washington, D.C. The lecture was eventually published, and to the surprise of its author, it prompted a storm of responses. In his paper, White argued that the marriage of science and technology in the nineteenth century led to the ecological crisis of the twentieth century: "Our present combustion of fossil fuels threatens to change the chemistry of the globe's atmosphere as a whole, with consequences which we are only beginning to guess. With the population explosion, the carcinoma of planless urbanism, the geological deposits of sewage and garbage, surely no creature other than man [*sic*] has ever managed to foul its nest in such short order."[1]

White did not end his examination with a discussion of technology. He also claimed that the framework that enabled the crisis was created by what he called "the Judeo-Christian tradition": "By gradual stages a loving and all-powerful God had created light and darkness, the heavenly bodies, the earth and all its plants, animals, birds, and fishes. Finally God created

---

[1] Lynn T. White Jr., "The Historical Roots of Our Ecological Crisis," *Science*, 155.3767 (March 10, 1967): 1204.

Adam. . . . God planned all of this explicitly for man's benefit and rule: no item in the physical creation had any purpose save to serve man's purpose. . . . By destroying pagan animism, Christianity made it possible to exploit nature in a mood of indifference."[2] Here White relied on the first creation story in Genesis 1:1–2:4, with its mandate to "rule" and "subdue" the earth and its creatures; he somehow missed the second creation story in Genesis 2:5-25, with its invitation to "till" and "keep" the earth.

White then made explicit his charge against Christianity: "As we now recognize, somewhat over a century ago, science and technology—hitherto quite separate activities—joined to give mankind powers which, to judge by many of the ecologic effects, are out of control. If so, Christianity bears a huge burden of guilt."[3] White's claim that the ecological crisis of the twentieth century (now continuing in the twenty-first century) can be traced to the biblical and theological framework of Christianity was grounded in the assumption that Christianity is a religion that, at its best, inspires indifference to the earth and, to its shame, sanctions domination and exploitation of the planet.

What interests the close reader of White's lecture and its subsequent publication is that he offered little evidence to support his claim. But, then, one wonders if his upbringing in a strict Calvinist church devoid of the sacramental and liturgical gifts of the earth shaped his view of Christianity. What surprises the reader of White's lecture more than fifty years after its publication is that, despite the absence of evidence, his claim continues to animate those who support it and those who disagree with it.[4]

---

[2] White, "Historical Roots of Our Ecological Crisis," 1205.

[3] White, "Historical Roots of Our Ecological Crisis," 1206.

[4] See *Religion and Ecological Crisis: The "Lynn White Thesis" at Fifty*, ed. Todd LeVasseur and Anna Peterson (New York: Routledge, 2017); Michael Paul Nelson and Thomas J. Sauer, "The Long Reach of Lynn White Jr.'s 'The His-

One wonders: Is it possible that those who support White simply take for granted his unsubstantiated assumption because it agrees with their own views of Christianity? Or is there some truth in White's claim that Christians have simply ignored the fate of the earth? But, then, what of more recent research suggesting that, for at least a thousand years, Christian communities did *not* view the earth as an inanimate object to exploit with indifference?

The Christ of Creation

Every Christmas, the gospel appointed for Mass during the Night is Luke 2:1-14, in which angels announce to a group of shepherds that a child born in Bethlehem is "Savior" and "Lord." Within its historical context, the announcement was startling since only one person, the Roman emperor, was widely acclaimed as the savior of the world and lord of lords. The tension between the political claim of the emperor and the announcement of the angels cannot be lost on us, for it provokes one to ask, "What kind of savior is the newborn, and for what does he save people?" While the Roman emperors claimed dominion over land and water and claimed their "right" to use or exploit them for their own purposes, we find in Jesus a loving familiarity with the earth and its many creatures. We do not hear of indifferent exploitation but rather thanksgiving to God for the earth and its many gifts. Indeed,

torical Roots of Our Ecologic Crisis,'" *Ecology & Evolution*, December 13, 2016, accessed on September 30, 2022, at https://ecoevocommunity.nature.com /posts/14041-the-long-reach-of-lynn-white-jr-s-the-historical-roots-of-our -ecologic-crisis; Bron Taylor, Gretel Van Wieren, and Bernard Daley Zaleha, "Lynn White Jr. and the Greening-of-Religion Hypothesis," *Conservation Biology* 30.5 (2016): 1000–1009; Michael S. Northcott, *Place, Ecology and the Sacred: The Moral Geography of Sustainable Communities* (London: Bloomsbury, 2015), 15–16; Richard Hoffmann, *An Environmental History of Medieval Europe* (Cambridge: Cambridge University Press, 2014), 85–91.

if we understand salvation as the *bestowal* of life, health, and wholeness in human and creaturely life, then the many stories of the gospels in which the natural world is invoked and blessed by Jesus can open an ecophilic reading of the New Testament.

As a complement to Luke's praise of the birth of a different kind of savior, a Savior who is in solidarity with all that is marginalized and oppressed by the powers and principalities of this world,[5] the gospel proclaimed on Christmas Day presents the Word of God as the agent of creation, that Word of God who has taken flesh in human form: "In the beginning was the Word, and the Word was with God, and the Word was God. He was in the beginning with God. *All things came into being through him, and without him not one thing came into being.* What has come into being in him was life."[6] In counterpoint to the first creation in Genesis 1, John announces that in Jesus one sees the cosmic Christ creating and, in his risen life, suffusing the earth with his life-giving presence.

In a similar vein, the second reading appointed for the solemnity of Our Lord Jesus Christ the King includes an early Christian hymn: "He is the image of the invisible God, the firstborn of all creation; for in him all things in heaven and on earth were created, things visible and invisible, whether thrones or dominions or rulers or powers—all things have been created through him and for him. He himself is before all things, and in him all things hold together."[7] In this hymn, one hears an echo of wisdom motifs in the Hebrew Scriptures: "The LORD by wisdom founded the earth"[8] and "When [the LORD] established the heavens, I [Wisdom] was there, . . . when he marked out the foundations of the earth, / then I was beside

---

[5] Luke 1:1-4; 4:14-21 (appointed for Ordinary Time 3, year C).

[6] John 1:1-4a; emphasis mine (appointed for Christmas Mass during the Day, years A, B, and C).

[7] Colossians 1:15-20 (appointed for Ordinary Time 15, year C).

[8] Proverbs 3:19.

him, like a master worker."[9] Indeed, the hymn holds together Christ as the active agent *of* creation and the first born *from* the creation. Through Christ and for him, all things—light; darkness; soil; water; vegetation; and a vast, diverse array of creatures—were brought to life and are held together in him. One wonders: Was this image of the cosmic-creating Christ simply lost on those who accepted at face value the notion that Christian faith and life are *ecomisia* (earth-hating)?

But, then, a careful reading of the gospels would reveal a complement to the cosmic Christologies of the New Testament letters. One cannot help but recognize that, in his public life, Jesus of Nazareth was fully engaged in the distinctive ecology of Palestine. He was baptized by John in the Jordan River and spent much of his adult life close to the Sea of Galilee, both bodies of fresh water teeming with life.[10] He was familiar with fish and fishing,[11] wine culture,[12] and various forms of soil.[13] He considered bread and fish good gifts of the earth.[14] He invited his disciples to anoint the sick with olive oil.[15] He spoke of care and protection for animals[16] and of God feeding the birds of the sky.[17] He was with wild animals in the wilderness[18] and was compared to a docile lamb.[19] The trees of ancient

[9] Proverbs 8:27, 29b-30a (appointed for Trinity Sunday, year C).

[10] Matthew 3:13-17; Mark 1:7-11; Luke 3:15-16, 21-22 (each text appointed, respectively, for the Baptism of the Lord in years A, B, and C).

[11] Luke 5:1-11 (appointed for Ordinary Time 5, year C); John 21:1-19 (appointed for Easter 3, year C).

[12] Mark 11:1-10; Mark 14:1–15:47 (appointed for Sunday of the Passion, year B); Matthew 20:1-16a (appointed for Ordinary Time 25, year A).

[13] Matthew 13:1-23 (appointed for Ordinary Time 15, year A).

[14] Matthew 7:9-11.

[15] Mark 6:7-13 (appointed for Ordinary Time 15, year B).

[16] John 10:1-18 (appointed for Easter 4, years A and B); see also Matthew 18:12-14; Luke 15:4-7.

[17] Matthew 6:24-34 (appointed for Ordinary Time 8, year A).

[18] Mark 1:12-13 (appointed for Lent 1, year B).

[19] John 1:29-34 (appointed for Ordinary Time 2, year A).

Palestine—the fig,[20] palm,[21] and sycamore[22]—entered his parables and encounters. Indeed, he spoke of himself as a life-giving vine.[23] Rather than use abstract and ethereal concepts more attuned to philosophy, his sayings and parables drew upon the rich agriculture of his homeland. The landscape in which he lived and ministered mattered to him and certainly mattered to those who composed the gospels in their descriptions of land, water, animals, birds, fish, flora, and weather.

One wonders: Is this the Christ contemporary Christian communities encounter today? Does his location in the landscape of Palestine as well as his cosmic, creating presence appear in homilies, sermons, hymn texts, and prayers? Or, as many theologians have noted, has the triumph of the therapeutic in the religions of North America drawn attention away from the fate of the earth and underscored an anthropocentric view of Christian spirituality that focuses solely on the individual's spiritual journey or growth in holiness?

A Mass of Creation?

From the practices and sayings of Jesus, there flowed into early Christian and monastic communities a form of worship that welcomed the gifts of the earth, a ritual gathering in which earth's materiality was clearly present. It was from these communities that contemporary assemblies have received their form of worship. Consider the fact that Christians, informed by the movement of the sun and moon, gather daily for prayer in the morning, at midday, in the evening, and at night. The church's sense of time is not governed by the market, schools,

[20] Luke 13:1-9 (appointed for Lent 3, year C).

[21] Matthew 21:1-11; Mark 11:1-10; Luke 19:28-40 (each text appointed, respectively, for Palm Sunday in years A, B, and C).

[22] Luke 9:1-10 (appointed for Ordinary Time 31, year C).

[23] John 15:1-17 (appointed for Easter 5 and Easter 6, year B).

or government but rather by sunset and sunrise, dawn and darkness: the day begins with sunset;[24] the week begins on Sunday (the day of resurrection, with its promise of new life), not Monday. Those entering Christian faith and life are washed in local water, are anointed with olive oil, and receive a bread fragment and a sip of wine in what are now called the sacraments of initiation. Had they lived in the early centuries of Christianity, they would have also received a cup of milk mixed with honey: a taste of the Promised Land.[25] Palm or other branches are dried and burned, their ashes marking the foreheads of the faithful. The towering paschal candle, created from the labor of bees and humans, signals the beginning of the Easter Vigil and the subsequent fifty days of paschal joy. The sharp odor of incense, an aromatic resin harvested in southern Arabia, permeates parish and monastic churches and cathedrals. Crowns of flowers, herbs, and greens adorn churches and, among the Eastern Orthodox, are placed on the heads of the wedding couple. Stone and wood are shaped into eucharistic tables. The words of Scripture, once inscribed on vellum, now on paper, are proclaimed in worship. Earth's gift of cotton and linen adorn the altar, the ministers, the newly baptized; a linen funeral pall is placed over the casket. The natural light of the sun, often interpreted metaphorically as the light of God's grace, shines through colored stained glass,

---

[24] With the Orthodox, Catholics and other Christian communions understand the liturgical day's beginning with sunset; thus, with dusk begins the solemnity of the Nativity, of the Epiphany, of Easter, of the Assumption. In this regard, the vast majority of Christians follow the Jewish pattern of keeping the day: from sunset to sunset (*not* from midnight to midnight or morning to morning).

[25] "The bishop gives thanks with regard to the mingled milk and honey which represents the promise God made to our fathers signified by the land flowing with milk and honey and fulfilled in the flesh of Christ which he gives us and by which believers are nourished like little children." "The Apostolic Tradition," in Lucien Deiss, CSSP, *The Springtime of the Liturgy*, trans. Matthew J. O'Connell (Collegeville, MN: Liturgical Press, 1979), 144.

the colors of the earth brightly illuminating the life of Christ, his blessed mother, the saints, and the martyrs who form the ancestors of the local assembly.

An ecological reading of the liturgy thus leads us to ask: Have Christians not been celebrating a Mass of Creation for two thousand years? After all, the sacramental center of Christian faith and life is utterly dependent on the gifts of the earth as the very *matter* through which God is revealed to humankind. "Flood, fire, the rock, the sea, the mountain . . . in all of them Israel touched the face of God, found help for discerning a way, moved toward the reign of justice and peace. . . . And then in Jesus, the Word of God is flesh."[26]

But, then, perhaps the earthy materiality of the Christian liturgy has been eclipsed at times because sacramental *efficacy*—how the sacraments work—has been emphasized at the expense of sacramental *signification*—what the earthy material of these actions offers in their richest, fullest sense.[27] An ecophilic perspective can thus focus one's attention on the significance of earth's presence in Christian faith and life by underscoring the claim made here: without the earth, there is no sacrament, no sacramental spirituality, no sacramental imagination. Again, we ask: Have Christians not been keeping a Mass of Creation for two thousand years, centered in the Christ, the firstborn of creation? And if we affirm that claim, would we not be drawn to care for and live in harmony with the earth and its many gifts and creatures?

In a mystic vision, the Seer of Patmos saw "the holy city, the new Jerusalem, coming down out of heaven from God" and "heard a loud voice from the throne saying, // 'See, the home of God is among mortals.' "[28] And, then, "the angel showed

---

[26] Bishops' Committee on the Liturgy, National Conference of Catholic Bishops, *Environment and Art in Catholic Worship* (Washington, DC: USCC, 1978), 2–3.

[27] Bishops' Committee on the Liturgy, *Environment and Art*, 14.

[28] Revelation 21:2-3 (appointed for Easter 5, year C).

me the river of the water of life, bright as crystal, flowing from the throne of God and of the Lamb . . . [and] the tree of life with its twelve kinds of fruit . . . and the leaves of the tree . . . for the healing of the nations."[29] In this vision, a point frequently eclipsed by an earth-transcending spirituality focused on entering heaven, the home of God is on earth. *Earth renewed is God's habitation*: a river flowing with the water of life, a tree producing healing leaves. Note that there is no temple. God's presence extends throughout the landscape to all creatures. There is no fear of matter and the need to escape into an otherworldly, incorporeal existence. God brings green space; fresh, flowing water; and a tree that heals. And it is in this space that the servants of God enter into the liturgy before the wounded yet living Lamb.[30]

Attention to One's Local Ecology

As we have seen, Benedict found a home by a river flowing with fresh water, a river teeming with life. Among the trees that grew on the side of the Subiacan ravine, one could find herbs, berries, and a seasonal array of vegetables. While Gregory refers to this region as a *deserti*,[31] paleoecologists suggest that fish, fruits, and other wild plants could sustain life, a hermit's life as he discerned his calling to be a monastic leader. In Gregory's stories about Benedict's sojourn in this "wild place," we can see that he knew the landscape in which he lived: a river flowing into a lake, bare rocky heights, a steep hillside, animals and birds, nettles and briars, aquifers, and a rough mountainside. There is wisdom to be gleaned in this

---

[29] Revelation 22:1, 2 (appointed for Easter 6, year C).

[30] Revelation 22:3 (appointed for Easter 6, year C).

[31] A "wilderness" or "desert"; *Dialogues* II.1.3. Terrence Kardong, OSB, speaks of it as a "wild place" in *The Life of St. Benedict by Gregory the Great: Translation and Commentary* (Collegeville, MN: Liturgical Press, 2009), 7.

familiarity with one's terrain: it is neither a stranger "out there" nor a collection of inanimate objects; the earthy place of one's existence becomes a prominent actor in one's life.

Can one care for, live in harmony with, and even love one's local habitat as a gift from God without knowing it well, without having a sense of place? "An environmental ethic needs to be based on a deep and abiding knowledge of the local environment. Individuals and communities become aware of the need for environmental sensitivity when they consciously choose to learn from and fall in love with a place."[32]

Of course, for the many people in North America who now live in urban and suburban centers, it can be a challenge to become aware of one's local habitat; much of the original landscape has been replaced by concrete, asphalt, and steel—by development, if not overdevelopment. In some places, water sources are obscured, orchards and forests are replaced by vast housing complexes, and fields are transformed into malls and parking lots. And yet, even in the midst of such overcrowding, one can search for the sources of one's water in aquifers, rivers, creeks, reservoirs, lakes, and mountain snowpack. One can protect and expand tree canopies and wetlands, prevent further loss of green corridors, and work to preserve urban and suburban parks from overdevelopment or neglect.

Knowing one's local ecology well also includes recognizing the sources of pollution that degrade the landscape and affect the well-being of humans and other creatures. In 1958, Olga Huskins wrote a letter to the *Boston Herald* in which she described the inordinate number of bird deaths on her property in Roxbury, Massachusetts, avian mortality she attributed to

[32] Abbot John Klassen, OSB, "The Rule of Benedict and Environmental Stewardship" (public lecture, Sustainability Summit, College of Saint Benedict/Saint John's University, 2004), at https://web.archive.org/web/2020080 9120950/https://www.csbsju.edu/sju-sustainability/about-us/benedictine -stewardship/values/klassen.

the recent aerial spraying of DDT in order to diminish the mosquito population. She sent a copy of the letter to her friend Rachel Carson, asking the marine biologist for the name of a federal agency where she could lodge her complaint. It was Huskins's attention to the bird deaths on her property and her letter to the *Boston Herald* that affirmed Carson's early investigation of the terrible effects of synthetic poisons and prompted the creation of her seminal work *Silent Spring*, published in 1962.[33]

From the publication of Carson's study and her warning concerning the effects of synthetic chemicals on plants, water, birds, fish, animals, and humans, there sprang to life the modern environmental movement in North America. Not unsurprisingly, Carson's study was met with fierce criticisms and denials from the chemical industry in the United States and Canada. And yet, President John Kennedy, the first Catholic president in U.S. history, asked members of his administration and his science advisory committee to study Carson's claims. In spring 1963, the committee report was published; its findings supported Carson's conclusion concerning the detrimental effects of pesticide toxicity. All this because one person was attentive to her local ecology, recognized its degradation, and called for assistance that led to its remediation.

Friendship with Other Creatures

We know that Benedict was also familiar with birds in his local habitat. Gregory mentions that the tempter, in the form of a little blackbird, sought to annoy the hermit and was banished when Benedict made the sign of the cross. Another

---

[33] In the introduction to her famous work, Rachel Carson noted the importance of Huskins's letter: Carson, *Silent Spring*, 40th anniversary ed. (New York: Houghton Mifflin, 2002), viii.

bird appears in Benedict's life: the raven he befriended and with whom he shared food and conversation.[34] To the skeptic of anything that looks even remotely "miraculous," this vignette may well appear as nothing more than simple fiction from an earlier and "unenlightened" age. But such skepticism seems to miss a salient point in the story: the friendship between humans and other creatures—Anthony of Egypt with his pig; Melangell of Wales and the rabbits who prayed with her; Giles of the Rhone Valley, the protector and friend of deer; Gertrude of Nivelles, who offered monastic hospitality to cats; Jerome of Bethlehem with a lion in his monastic enclave; Columba of Ireland and salmon. To the indigenous nations of North America, none of this seems the least bit odd; after all, the salmon, the eagle, the wolf, and a host of other nonhuman creatures continue to communicate the values and practices of a particular community, they are manifestations of the Creator's guidance, and they play significant roles in teaching ethics.

In the sixth century, the Christian philosopher and Neoplatonist Pseudo-Dionysius the Areopagite promoted the notion that celestial and ecclesiastical realms of existence are ordered in a hierarchical manner: the Holy Trinity at the summit of the celestial sphere and "ordinary" angels at the base, bishops at the apex of the ecclesiastical sphere with "unwashed" people preparing for baptism at the bottom. Such stratifications inspired the Great Chain of Being, a vision of all existence ordered into superior and inferior ranks, from God downward to minerals. In between humans and rocks, one finds animals and, within the animal "category," its own hierarchy: from the lion downward to the oyster and sea worm.

The stories of monastic friendship with other creatures seem to depart from this rigid ranking of existence into superior and inferior forms. Gregory reports that Benedict conversed with

---

[34] *Dialogues* II.8.3; see pp. 63–66.

the raven, and the raven protected Benedict and others from harm. What one discerns in these stories is not so much miracle or fiction as it is the recognition that all creation exists in an *interdependent*, rather than an autonomous, manner. In these stories, one begins to move away from an anthropocentric view of life focused solely on human need and toward an ecocentric view that can sustain a harmonious relationship with other creatures and the landscapes shared by humans and other-than-human beings.

Indeed, such friendship, along with the condemnation of cruelty, has been clearly articulated by Pope Francis in his encyclical on the environment: "Every act of cruelty towards any creature is contrary to human dignity. . . . Everything is related, and we human beings are united as brothers and sisters on a wonderful pilgrimage, woven together by the love God has for each of his creatures and which also unites us in fond affection with brother sun, sister moon, brother river and mother earth."[35] Again, interdependence nudges out atomistic autonomy. Thus, it is good to remember that the "name" of the first human in the biblical story of creation was *'adam*, meaning "earth creature"—one creature drawn from earth's soil among many others in a common landscape. And we rightly keep in mind that monastic friendship with birds, fish, and animals stood in stark contrast to the savagery of imperial Rome, in which thousands of animals were slaughtered in arenas throughout the empire solely for the sake of entertainment: cruel bloodshed as sport.[36]

---

[35] *Laudato Si'* 92. Anatoly A. R. Aseneta argues that considerable strides on care for nonhuman animals were made in the encyclical but also adds that such care needs to address industrial food processing, the use of animals as clothing, and their use in biomedical research; Aseneta, "*Laudato Si'* on Non-Human Animals," *Journal of Moral Theology* 6.2 (2017): 230–45.

[36] One is mindful of the terrible cost of industrialized food production in North America on animals, humans, and the environment. See Mary McGann, RSCJ, *The Meal That Reconnects: Eucharistic Eating and the Global Food Crisis* (Collegeville, MN: Liturgical Press, 2020), 55–122.

Here we suggest that Benedict's awareness of his local ecology and his friendship with a nonhuman creature are a source of monastic wisdom for the present. Rather than ignorance of one's habitat, attention to the local ecology can become a source of Christian thanksgiving for its natural grace and life-giving qualities. The invocation of one's local waters in the blessing of baptismal waters is an example of such thanksgiving. Attention to one's natural habitat can also lead to Christian lament where land or water is degraded. Monastic transformation of an infested swamp into a flowing river or fertile field was one instance in which the grace of labor transformed nature. The contemporary cleaning and subsequent "healing" of contaminated land and water sources—Superfund sites—at the behest of the Environmental Protection Agency is in continuity with ancient monastic care for the land and rivers that supported life. Volunteer cleanups of degraded creeks, wetlands, and prairies complement the work of governmental agencies.

Humility

We know from the Rule that the virtue of humility is of primary importance in monastic and Christian life. However, it is not a virtue widely promoted in Western European and North American cultures. The individual is preeminent, and the individual's needs and ambitions are of central concern. Investment in the self alone tends to trump what we have seen in the life of Benedict: investment in others for the sake of a healthy community. At the same time, American culture rewards "winners," women and men who are self-made "successes." Those who choose divestment from privilege for the sake of others are easily viewed with skepticism. Thus, to speak of humility as a virtue to be pursued in a culture that prizes individual achievement, winning at all cost, may seem quite odd.

Yet this dimension of monastic wisdom is critical when pursuing a relationship with human and nonhuman others as well as one's landscape. We know that the root meaning of humility is derived from *humus* (earthiness, being of the earth). Humus is the dark organic matter in soil that is created through the process of decomposition. The virtue of humus, of humility, is in the recognition that humans and most other creatures possess a common origin in the soil: from either a biblical or an evolutionary perspective. As Benedict and many other monastic leaders knew well, the opposite of humility is pride: pretentiousness, selfish ambition, exercising control over others for one's personal gain, imagining oneself or one's group or one's species to be above others and thus morally superior to them. By way of contrast, "humility keeps the monk close to the earth."[37]

In his comment on the twelfth step of humility, Benedict writes that "at the Work of God, in the oratory, the monastery or the garden, on a journey or in the field, or anywhere else" and "whether he sits, walks or stands, [the monk's] head must be bowed and his gaze be fixed on the earth."[38] Clearly Benedict is speaking of the manner in which a monk or nun visually demonstrates humility. But note the instruction to have one's head bowed *with eyes toward the ground*. Can we recognize in this instruction not only a spiritual maxim but also a physical one: look to the ground, the place of your origin, the soil upon which you stand? From a Christian perspective, the virtue of humility can free the soul to recognize its natural relationship with God and with the earth: humans are one with the soil, with its many water sources, with plants and trees, birds, fish,

---

[37] Monastery of Christ in the Desert, "Sustainable Stewardship," *Monastery of Christ in the Desert*, 2022, accessed on November 15, 2022, at https://christdesert.org/about/sustainable-stewardship/.

[38] RB 7.63.

and animals. "The human choice is to live within the constraints of creaturehood."[39]

Simplicity

Benedict speaks of constraint in the Rule: plain clothing, simple food, and an equitable sharing of what is needed to live. In contrast to the wealthy Christians of Rome who overlooked the needs of the many poor, Benedict promoted a life marked by the voluntary embrace of simplicity, a life marked by living with the essentials: shelter, clothing, rudimentary medical care, and a modest diet drawn from the local landscape. Inspired by the equitable sharing of the first followers of Jesus,[40] the Rule guaranteed that all members of the community would have sufficient nourishment to sustain healthy living: a noticeable contrast to the world Benedict left behind in Rome, where the few had much and the many had very little.

While he may have experienced a measure of well-padded comfort earlier in life, he divested himself of such privilege when he entered the Subiacan ravine as a hermit. One wonders if Benedict, "who despised the glory of the world as if it were a dried out flower,"[41] discovered the natural habitat of Subiaco to be an ever-flowing gift from God. If this were the case, he would not be alone. After all, others who were guided by the Rule—Godric of Finchale, Walafrid Strabo, Bruno of Grande Chartreuse, and Hildegard of Bingen—recognized the natural landscape in which they lived as sacred ground that called for careful stewardship. Having let go of the desire for material possessions, political and ecclesial power, and social status, Benedict was little different from other monastic leaders who prescribed or proposed an uncluttered life.

[39] Klassen, "Rule of Benedict and Environmental Stewardship."
[40] Acts 2:44-45; 4:32-37; RB 33.
[41] *Dialogues* II.1.5.

For those who live in well-padded comfort today, the Rule serves as a challenge to what many consider "normal" in society. For instance, a capitalist economic system values private ownership and the accumulation of wealth or capital for the individual, family, business, or corporation. The more accumulated the better, thus leading a society to reward those with wealth and ignore or disdain those challenged by poverty. At the same time, when the accrual of wealth becomes the norm, all other things become ordered to that goal, frequently with disastrous results. No wonder, then, that pollution, degradation of the earth, and the loss of species appear to be an "acceptable cost" in gaining greater profit. The thirst for greater material wealth, induced by sophisticated advertising in order to drive sales and investment, quickly leads to what the medievals considered the vice of avarice or greed—materialism writ large.

In a society wedded to capitalist materialism, the monastic practices of common ownership, land stewardship, and the provision of shelter, clothing, food, and medical care for all may well appear quixotic and impractical. But then one wonders: Should not the monastic practice of ensuring that no one is in want be the *first* principle that orders a society's primary responsibility: to ensure that its people and its land flourish? While North Americans are quick to praise freedom from governmental restraint, individual rights, self-sufficiency, and unlimited growth, such concerns easily overlook or ignore what serves the common good and ecological flourishing. In a time when the earth is suffering with little restraint in harmful fossil fuel consumption and the illusion of ever-increasing growth predicated on earth-degrading practices, monastic insistence on moderation, the control of consumption, and careful stewardship of land and water sources serves as both social criticism and an alternative that can sustain human and ecological thriving.

It should not surprise us that Pope Francis has pointed out this dreadful tendency in modern society: to view humans, creatures of the earth, and the earth itself as disposable commodities. In a culture that accepts disposability as a norm, humankind, other creatures, and the earth all suffer: they are similarly used up and then tossed away. The exploitation of the earth is little different from the exploitation of human beings; indeed, the two go hand in hand. "Each year hundreds of millions of tons of waste are generated, much of it non-biodegradable, highly toxic and radioactive, from homes and businesses, from construction and demolition sites, from clinical, electronic and industrial sources. The earth, our home, is beginning to look more and more like an immense pile of filth. . . . Industrial waste and chemical products utilized in cities and agricultural areas can lead to bioaccumulation in the organisms of the local population, even when levels of toxins in those places are low. Frequently no measures are taken until after people's health has been irreversibly affected."[42] The commodification of human life and the life of the earth participates in what Pope Francis calls a "throwaway culture."[43] Those who are impoverished, uneducated, and considered fit only for menial labor are easily thrown away no differently than forests are cut down, wetlands are developed, and water sources are polluted or privatized for corporate profit. "The deterioration of the environment and of society affects the most vulnerable people on the planet."[44]

---

[42] *Laudato Si'* 21.

[43] "Pope Francis expresses concern for those who are 'thrown away' through human trafficking, degrading living conditions, refugee status, unemployment, and for other reasons in which people find themselves excluded from the social arena." Lucia Silecchia, "*Laudato Si'* and the Tragedy of a 'Throwaway Culture,'" in *Catholic University of America Columbus School of Law Legal Studies*, research paper no. 2017-2 (Washington, DC: Catholic University of America, 2017), 4.

[44] *Laudato Si'* 48.

" 'Tis a gift to be simple," wrote Joseph Brackett, a member of the Shakers, an eighteenth-century utopian, egalitarian community that practiced communal living and a commitment to peace.[45] The monastic virtue of simplicity, of living with less, of living in such a manner that supports the flourishing of life, land, air, and water, invites responsible Catholics, other Christians, and all those concerned with the fate of the earth and its inhabitants to resist the dangerous call for continued economic growth and its current exploitation of the planet. "The Benedictine virtue of frugality offers us an alternative vision of sustainable consumption based not on want but on *essential need*."[46]

Christ in the Desert

The Italian authors of the 2016 application requesting World Heritage status for early medieval monastic communities acknowledge that these monastic complexes fit into the natural environment in a harmonious manner, "providing a valuable message for the contemporary society and for the future generations."[47] Such fitting into the natural environment is seen clearly in the Monastery of Christ in the Desert located in northern New Mexico, a monastic complex situated between the Chama River and the reddish-and-yellowed hills of the Mesa de Los Viejos. "From the moment the first monks arrived in 1964, the beauty of the Chama River Canyon has continually inspired prayer and praise. It seemed desirable for the monks

[45] Roger L. Hall, *Simple Gifts: A Great American Folk Song* (Stoughton, MA: Pine Tree Productions, 2014).

[46] Klassen, "Rule of Benedict and Environmental Stewardship"; emphasis mine.

[47] Permanent Delegation of Italy to UNESCO, "The Cultural Landscape of the Benedictine Settlements in Medieval Italy," March 18, 2016, accessed on July 16, 2022, at https://whc.unesco.org/en/tentativelists/6107/.

to learn to simply fit into a natural environment that was itself already praising God for such glory."[48] Rather than constructing buildings that stood apart from the local ecology or even overwhelmed it with their monumentality, the monks have used the natural gifts of the region in such a way that the monastic complex blends into the river canyon and west-facing cliffs.

Drawing on ancient building materials, the monastic complex has been constructed with adobe, a mudbrick formed by the mixing of sand, silt, and clay with water and straw. Indeed, adobe has proved to be one of the strongest natural materials in construction, with the added benefit of holding the heat of the sun in colder temperatures as well as protecting inhabitants from high heat in the summer. The use of local and inexpensive straw bales serves as a primary form of insulation. The ceilings of the monastic complex follow the traditional use of local timber, mostly ponderosa pine, formed into *vigas*, the thick wooden beams that support the roof. Fallen and prudently harvested pine from the canyon serves as the source of the vigas as well as other furnishings throughout the complex.

Drawing on early monastic practice, the buildings have been constructed in such a way as to garner as much natural light as possible. Electricity is derived from an array of solar panels that store energy in batteries; it is one of the largest solar fields in the state. Water is drawn from the Chama River and supplies a water system that is completely self-sufficient. Wastewater is diverted into a constructed wetland of cattails, reeds, flowers, and bulrushes that break down waste and chemicals through the use of natural microorganisms. Thus, with careful stewardship, local adobe, trees, sunlight, water, and plants sustain the common life of the monastery. At the same time, the local ecology, "already praising God" for its beauty,[49] is honored and

---

[48] Monastery of Christ in the Desert, "Sustainable Stewardship."
[49] Monastery of Christ in the Desert, "Sustainable Stewardship."

cared for by a monastery committed to sustainable stewardship. There is much practical wisdom alive in this and other monastic communities where a commitment to wise stewardship moves beyond rhetoric and becomes action.[50]

But, we ask, what has prompted this monastic community to honor its local ecology and live in harmonious relationship with land, water, and forest? "The Benedictine charism, notable for simplicity, humility, stability, and hospitality, is especially well suited to sustainable stewardship of the natural environment."[51] It is the values and practices of the Rule, itself a reflection of the gospels, that animate such ecological wisdom and inspire an ecophilic spirit. The virtue of simplicity avoids excesses that damage the environment. Humility, or *humus*, keeps one's eyes on the ground, the soil, the place of one's origin. The vow of stability prevents constant movement and the tendency toward disposability. In this monastic community, a "throwaway" culture is mitigated. Living in and knowing one's natural habitat inspires a love for the land given by God and entrusted to human stewardship. Welcoming novices, oblates, and guests directs the vision of the community to the future and how an ethic of care in the present will ensure human and ecological stability for generations to come.

Yet such concern for the local ecology radiates outward from the practice of daily prayer and the celebration of the Mass, at whose center is Jesus Christ, the One through whom all things came into being;[52] the One who sustains all things;[53] the

---

[50] Jason Brown offers an illuminating study of select North American monastic communities engaged in sustainable stewardship in "The 'Greening' of Christian Monasticism and the Future of Monastic Landscapes in North America," *Religions* 10.432 (2019): 1–12. See also Josep-Maria Mallarach, Josep Corcó, and Thymio Papayannis, "Christian Monastic Communities Living in Harmony with the Environment: An Overview of Positive Trends and Best Practices," *Studia Monastica* 56 (2014): 353–91.

[51] Monastery of Christ in the Desert, "Sustainable Stewardship."

[52] John 1:3.

[53] Hebrews 1:3.

firstborn of all creation;[54] the new creation;[55] the true vine;[56] the light;[57] the bright morning star;[58] and the living water.[59] While Christology and ethics are frequently separated in theological study and Christian spirituality, the enduring monastic practice of *ora et labora*, "prayer and work," can hold the two together. And it is the holding of these two together that grounds care for the earth within a community gathered around an earthy ritual.

Said another way, Jesus will teach that the greatest commandment is twofold: to love God with all one's being and to love one's neighbor as oneself. Of course the command is twofold; one leads to the other. We cannot say we love God and hold disdain or distance from our neighbor in need. What we are coming to learn, at times ever so slowly, is that the new neighbor in need is the earth and all its creatures. And in that learning, we can be guided by those who left a world marked by wastefulness and degradation, who entered the wilderness and, there, took up the work to restore all things—*all* things—in Christ.

[54] Colossians 1:15.

[55] 2 Corinthians 5:17.

[56] John 15:1.

[57] John 1:5.

[58] Revelation 22:16.

[59] John 4:14.

7

The Land Is in the Church

I first caught sight of Saint John's Abbey Church in a black-and-white photograph my mother showed me in 1965, a photograph used in a graduate course she was taking on American architecture, part of the curriculum in art education she was pursuing at the time. She was amazed by the daring of the monks who sponsored the building of a church that embodied a vision so ahead of its time. Marcel Breuer, the Hungarian-born architect commissioned by the abbey, broke many of the canons of North American church architecture and created a space striking in its difference yet still in continuity with the traditional centers of Catholic and monastic worship. Dedicated in 1961, the abbey church preceded the Second Vatican Council, a council whose proceedings promoted significant changes in the worship and worldview of the church: a global church that engaged the modern world and embraced "the joys and the hopes, the griefs and the anxieties of this age, especially of those who are poor or in any way afflicted."[1]

Ten years after seeing that photograph of the abbey church, I was a student in the School of Theology at Saint John's University, and, in another ten years, I was teaching in the seminary of the Archdiocese of Saint Paul and Minneapolis. In 1986,

---

[1] Pastoral Constitution on the Church in the Modern World: *Gaudium et Spes*, 1.

I asked my friend Amelia, an English Catholic, if she and her daughters wanted to join me for Sunday Mass at the abbey. She responded positively, as she was curious to see the church, having never been to Collegeville but aware of its architectural significance. A few days before our Sunday drive, she called and asked if her husband, Paul, a professor of geology, could join us. Within two minutes of arriving on the campus, she indicated that during his undergraduate studies at an English university, he had departed from the practice of the faith. As he once told me, it was fine to raise their children "with religion" since religion could offer a moral vision, but for him, he simply had many other things to do. Indeed, he was working on a new survey of the geology and topography of Minnesota, appointed to this position by the governor. I asked myself, "Why would this man, whose intellectual maturity was shaped by the Scientific Revolution and the Enlightenment's criticism of religion, why would he be interested in visiting a Benedictine abbey?" When I asked what prompted his desire to join us, he said he was simply interested in getting out of town and visiting another Minnesota landmark.

We arrived just as Mass was beginning so we hurried into the church and found our place in one of the pews. Sitting quietly after communion, I noticed that Paul was not with us. Indeed, we searched for him for some time—not anxious, just wondering what had happened to him. At last I found him standing in the balcony, in the top row, gazing on one of the colored windows that forms the massive honeycomb wall of glass. I was a surprised and a bit confused by what I saw. It was clear that Paul had been weeping: he was sniffling and his eyes were watery.

"Is something out of sorts?" I asked him.

He cleared his throat and in his crisp British accent said, "Oh no, oh no, just fine. But . . ." He paused and then said, ever so slowly, "*I know just about everything here. I know just about everything in this space* and, truth be told, I can't believe what I see."

"Paul," I said, flummoxed, "are you speaking metaphysically?"

He let out a snort and said gently, "No, you goose. I am talking about this building, this church. Samuel, don't you see? Minnesota is in the church. *The land is in the church.* Look: The granite from Cold Spring. The glazed brick. The dark wood from Chatfield. That great pile of concrete. The white oak from what I assume is the abbey forest. The Bak glass.[2] And the water—the water in that gurgling font must be from a local source." Then, showing his sweet ignorance of Benedictine history, he continued, "I mean, I had no idea the monks or the architect or whoever would draw so much from the land . . . here, here in this space."

Well, perhaps in the end he was speaking metaphysically, since this chance encounter with a monastic space, one that welcomed and thus honored the local ecology, participated in his return to the practice of the faith not as a teenager, when he set it aside, but as an adult who had been surprisingly, unexpectedly evangelized—yes, *evangelized*—by stone and brick, glass and wood. He was evangelized not by singing, not by preaching, not by praying, not by communing, but by the space itself, the house in which the church has always welcomed the gifts of the earth—that is, if one has the eyes to see them.

Ever since this epiphany in 1986, I have wondered if worshipers and their leaders recognize the presence of their local ecology in their churches, chapels, and oratories—if, in fact, there is anything of the local habitat present. I know that the water that flows into the parish font where I serve comes from the rain that hardens into snowpack in the Cascade Mountain Range, which then melts into the Green River, the immediate source of our water supply. Yet global warming is actually

---

[2] A reference to Bronislaw Bak, the Saint John's University faculty member who led monks, students, and volunteers in creating the many hexagonal windows that form the glass wall of Saint John's Abbey church.

melting the mountainous snowpacks that fill the reservoirs and rivers; we are losing the waters that used to flow in a plentiful manner throughout the region. The beams in the ceiling are constructed of cedar, a wood prized by indigenous communities for millennia because of its durability and beauty. Yet the cedar beams connect this community to the region's tragic history of broken treaties, sequestration of the indigenous population on reservations, and the unchecked harvesting of precious wood—harvesting that has removed the abundant undergrowth that has served as home to many birds and animals, undergrowth that in the past mitigated flooding but now no longer does. Through the glass doors of this parish church, one can see the majestic glacial summit of Mount Rainier. Yet we now know that the glaciers are disappearing at an alarming rate due to global warming. They are melting before our eyes.

In this study of early Christian and early Benedictine earth awareness and care for land and water, I have suggested that there is a good measure of ecological wisdom, a wisdom expressed in liturgical, sacramental, and monastic values and practices. I have suggested that there is an inextricable link between loving God and loving the neighbor in need, "neighbor" understood here as humankind, other-than-human creatures, and the earth itself, what we might call the new "poor and afflicted." In their pastoral statement on the environmental crisis, the United States Conference of Catholic Bishops notes concern for a "natural ecology and a social ecology," rightly claiming that it is the poor and vulnerable who suffer most from environmental blight.[3] It would seem, then, that care for the earth cannot be separated from advocacy for those most

---

[3] USCCB, *Renewing the Earth: An Invitation to Reflection and Action on the Environment in Light of Catholic Social Teaching* (Washington, DC: USCC, 1992), accessed on December 15, 2022, at https://www.usccb.org/resources/renewing-earth.

directly affected by pollution, chemical poisoning of land and water, and global warming.

It is worth remembering that early monastic communities were not self-enclosed fortresses oblivious to the reality of human suffering that surrounded them. Rather, the monastic virtue and practice of hospitality prompted monks and nuns to welcome the hungry, the sick, and those fleeing the violence of this world into monastic centers of stability and safety. Here the poor and the afflicted could find refuge. I wonder: Is it any different today? That is, are the people who gather in monasteries, parish churches, chapels, and oratories called not only to care for what the liturgy claims is God's earth, God's first gift of grace, but also to support those who suffer the most from environmental blight, a degradation of the earth largely caused by human action, if not human greed?

To our medieval ancestors in the faith, the world was a sacramental presence, a world that reveals God's presence through physical and tangible signs. The Enlightenment of the eighteenth century rendered the earth a subject of scientific exploration, an exploration from which many have benefited in terms of understanding earth's origins, its long development over billions of years, and its many interrelated systems of life. But all that exploration eclipsed and even ridiculed the vision of the creation as flowing from the creative power of a benevolent God. Perhaps, then, early Christian hymns, an earthy liturgy, and the monastic vision of the land as gift that asks for wise stewardship might just lead to a re-enchantment of the earth and the many lives it holds.

The Cistercian monk Thomas Merton once wrote that "Christianity is not so much a body of doctrine as the revelation of a Mystery."[4] And what is that Mystery?

---

[4] Thomas Merton, *Seasons of Celebration: Meditations on the Cycle of Liturgical Feasts* (Notre Dame, IN: Ave Maria Press, 1950), 81.

> I heard a loud voice . . . saying,
>> "See, the home of God is among mortals.
>> [God] will dwell with them . . .
> and . . . be their God."
>
> Then the angel showed me the river of the water of life, bright as crystal, flowing from the throne of God and of the Lamb. . . . On either side of the river is the tree of life with its twelve kinds of fruit, producing its fruit each month; and the leaves of the tree are for the healing of the nations.[5]

God's home is here on earth, where a river flows pure and clean and the tree of life bears fruit for the healing of the nations, bears fruit for nothing less than the healing of the earth and its many creatures.

[5] Revelation 21:3, 7; 22:1-2.

Bibliography

Primary Sources

"The Apostolic Tradition." In Lucien Deiss, *The Springtime of the Liturgy*, translated by Matthew J. O'Connell. Collegeville, MN: Liturgical Press, 1979.

Athanasius. "Life of Saint Antony." In *Ancient Christian Writers*, edited by Johannes Quasten and Joseph Plumpe and translated by Robert Meyer. Vol. 10. Westminster, MD: Newman Press, 1950.

Augustine of Hippo. *Explanation of the Psalms*. In *Nicene and Post-Nicene Fathers*, edited by Philip Schaff and Arthur Cleveland. Vol. 8. New York: Cosimo Classics, 2007.

Chronicon Sublacense (AA. 593–1369). Edited by Raffaello Morghen and translated by Arturo Carucci. Subiaco: Edizione Monastero S. Scolastica, 1991.

Chronicon Vulternense del Monaco Giovanni. Edited by Vincenzo Frederici. Rome: Istituto Storico Italiano, 1925.

Clement of Alexandria. "Exhortation to the Heathen." In *The Ante-Nicene Fathers: Fathers of the Second Century*, edited by Alexander Roberts and James Donaldson. Vol. 2. New York: Charles Scribner's Sons, 1899.

Clement of Alexandria. "Hymn to Christ the Teacher." In Lucien Deiss, *The Springtime of the Liturgy*, translated by Matthew J. O'Connell. Collegeville, MN: Liturgical Press, 1979.

Clement of Rome. "Letter to the Corinthians." In *Early Christian Writings*, edited by Andrew Louth and translated by Maxwell Staniforth. London and New York: Penguin, 1987.

"The Didache or Teaching of the Twelve Apostles." In Lucien Deiss, *The Springtime of the Liturgy*, translated by Matthew J. O'Connell. Collegeville, MN: Liturgical Press, 1979.

Diognetus. "Epistle to Diognetus." In *Early Christian Fathers*, edited and translated by Cyril C. Richardson. New York: Touchstone, 1953.

Flaccus, Quintus Horatius. *The Epistles of Horace*. Translated by David Ferry. New York: Farrar, Straus and Giroux, 2001.

Frontinus. *De Aquaeductu Urbis Romae*. Edited and translated by R. H. Rodgers. Cambridge: Cambridge University Press, 2004.

Gregory of Catino. *Il Regesto di Farfa*. In Benjamin J. Graham, "Profile of a Plant: The Olive in Early Medieval Italy, 400–900 CE," PhD diss. Ann Arbor: University of Michigan, 2014.

Gregory the Great. *Dialogues: Tome II*. Edited by Adalbert de Vogüé and translated by Paul Antin. Vol. 260 in *Sources Chrétiennes*. Paris: Éditions du CERF, 1979.

Hildegard of Bingen. *Liber Vitae Meritorum*. In Heinrich Schipperges, *The World of Hildegard of Bingen: Her Life, Times, and Visions*, translated by John Cumming. Collegeville, MN: Liturgical Press, 1998.

Josephus. *The Jewish War: Books IV–VII*. Translated by H. St. J. Thackeray. Cambridge: Harvard University Press, 1979.

Justin Martyr. "Dialogue with Trypho." In *The Ante-Nicene Fathers: Fathers of the Second Century*, edited by Marcus Dods and George Reith and translated by Philip Schaff. Vol. 1. Buffalo: Christian Literature Publishing, 1885.

Justin Martyr. "First Apology." In Lucien Deiss, *The Springtime of the Liturgy*, translated by Matthew J. O'Connell. Collegeville, MN: Liturgical Press, 1979.

Ovid. *Fasti*. Translated by James G. Frazer. Cambridge: Harvard University Press, 1931.

"The Passion of Perpetua and Felicity." In Jennifer A. Rea and Liz Clarke, *Perpetua's Journey: Faith, Gender, and Power in the Roman Empire*. New York: Oxford University Press, 2018.

Paul the Deacon. *History of the Langobards*. Translated by William D. Foulke. Philadelphia: University of Pennsylvania, 1907.

Paulus Fabius Maximus. "Letter of Paulus Fabius Maximus and Decrees by Asians Concerning the Provincial Calendar." In Frederick W. Danker, *Benefactor: Epigraphic Study of a Graeco-Roman and New Testament Semantic Field*. St. Louis: Clayton Publishing, 1982.

"Protoevangelium of James." In *The Infancy Gospels of James and Thomas*, translated by Ronald F. Hock. Santa Rosa: Polebridge Press, 1996.

Il Regesto Sublacense dell'undecimo Secolo. Edited by Guido Levi and Leone Allodi. Roma: Reale Società Romana di Storia Patria, 1885.

RB 1980: The Rule of St. Benedict in Latin and English with Notes. Edited by Timothy Fry. Collegeville, MN: Liturgical Press, 1981.

Strabo, Walafrid. "Hortulus: On the Cultivation of Gardens." In *A Benedictine Reader: 530–1530*, edited by Hugh Feiss, Ronald E. Pepin, and Maureen O'Brien. Collegeville, MN: Liturgical Press, 2019.

Suetonius. "The Life of Domitian." In *Lives of the Caesars*, translated by J. C. Rolfe. Vol. II. Cambridge: Harvard University Press, 1914.

Sulpitius Severus. "The Life of St. Martin of Tours." In *Early Christian Lives*, edited and translated by Carolinne White. London and New York: Penguin, 1998.

Tertullian. *On Baptism*. Edited and translated with introduction and commentary by Ernest Evans. London: SPCK, 1964.

Vitruvius Pollio, Marcus. *The Ten Books on Architecture*. Translated by Morris Hicky Morgan. New York: Dover, 1960.

Scripture and Ritual Texts

The Holy Bible. The New Revised Standard Version Bible. National Council of the Churches of Christ in the United States of America, 1989.

Lectionary for Mass. Collegeville, MN: Liturgical Press, 2002.

The Roman Missal. Third Typical Edition. Totowa, NJ: Catholic Book Publishing, 2011.

The Book of Common Prayer 1979. New York: Church Publishing, 1979.

Secondary Sources

Alikin, Valeriy A. *The Earliest History of the Christian Gathering: Origin, Development and Content of the Christian Gathering in the First to Third Centuries*. Leiden and Boston: Brill, 2010.

Aseneta, Anatoly A. R. "*Laudato Si'* on Non-Human Animals." *Journal of Moral Theology* 6.2 (2017): 230–45.

Ashby, Thomas. *The Roman Campagna in Classical Times*. London: Ernest Benn, 1927.

Auguet, Roland. *Cruelty and Civilization: The Roman Games*. New York: Routledge, 1994.

Bergant, Dianne. *The Earth Is the Lord's: The Bible, Ecology, and Worship*. Collegeville, MN: Liturgical Press, 1998.

Bishops' Committee on the Liturgy, National Conference of Catholic Bishops. *Environment and Art in Catholic Worship*. Washington, DC: United States Catholic Conference, 1978.

Branciani, Luchina. "Origine e sviluppo dell'eremitismo nella valle Sublacense." In *Le Valli dei Monaci*, edited by Letizia Pani Ermini, 585–635. Spoleto: Centro Italiano di Studi sull'Alto Medioevo, 2012.

Bratton, Susan. *Environmental Values in Christian Art*. Albany: State University of New York Press, 2008.

Brown, Jason. "The 'Greening' of Christian Monasticism and the Future of Monastic Landscapes in North America." *Religions* 10.432 (2019): 1–12.

Büntgen, Ulf, Willy Tegel, Kurt Nicolussi, Michael McCormick, David Frank, Valerie Trouet, Jed O. Kaplan, Franz Herzig, Karl-Uwe Heussner, Heinz Wanner, Jürg Luterbacher, and Jan Esper. "2500 Years of European Climate Variability and Human Susceptibility." *Science* 331 (February 2011): 578–82.

Carletti, Sandro. *The Catacombs of Priscilla*. Translated by Alice Mulhern. Vatican City: Pontifical Commission for Sacred Archaeology, 1982.

Carosi, Gabriele Paolo. "Note di storia della communità monastica sublacenese: La stampa a Subiaco." In *I monasteri benedettini di Subiaco*, edited by Claudio Giumelli, 203–16. Milan: Silvana Editoriale, 2002.

Carrara, Claudio. "Calcareous Tufa Deposits of the Aniene Valley between Vallepietra and Mandela-Vicovaro." *Italian Journal of Quaternary Sciences* 19 (2006): 19–44.

Carson, Rachel. *Silent Spring*. 40th anniversary ed. New York: Houghton Mifflin, 2002.

Cavaliere, M. G. Fiore. *Sublaqueum—Subiaco: Tra Nerone a S. Benedetto*. Rome: Quattro D Editrice, 1994.

Claiborne, Robert. *The Roots of English: A Reader's Handbook of Word Origins*. New York: Times Books/Random House, 1989.

Crossan, John Dominic. *God and Empire: Jesus Against Rome, Then and Now*. New York: HarperOne, 2007.

Dawson, Ashley. *Extinction: A Radical History*. New York: OR Books, 2016.

Deming, David. "The Aqueducts and Water Supply of Ancient Rome." *Ground Water* 58.1 (January/February 2020): 152–61.

D'Orefice, Maurizio, Silvana Falcetti, Paolo Moretti, Marco Pantaloni, Rita Pichezzi, and Anna Scalise. "Un territorio da (ri)scoprire: L'alta Valle del fiume Aniene." *Bollettino della Societa Geologica Italiana* 102 (January 2014): 101–18.

Dubos, René. "Franciscan Conservation versus Benedictine Stewardship." In *Ecology and Religion in History*, edited by David and Eileen Spring, 114–36. New York: Harper & Row, 1974.

Dunkle, Brian P. *Enchantment and Creed in the Hymns of Ambrose of Milan*. Oxford: Oxford University Press, 2016.

Ermini, Letizia Pani. "Subiaco all'epoca di S. Benedetto: Note di topografia." *Benedictina* 28 (1981): 69–80.

Fabbi, Simone. "Geology of the Northern Simbruini Mountains." *Journal of Maps* 12.1 (2016): 441–52.

Fabbi, Simone, Riccardo Cestari, and Rita Maria Pichezzi. "The 'Subiaco Stone' and the Early Studies on the Carbonate Successions of the Upper Aniene Valley." *Rendiconti Società Geologica Italiana* 44 (2018): 15–21.

Ferngren, Gary. *Medicine and Health Care in Early Christianity*. Baltimore: Johns Hopkins University Press, 2009.

"Flora." *Parco Naturale Regionale Monti Simbruini*, accessed on June 15, 2021, http://www.parks.it/parco.monti.simbruini/par.php.

Fox, Matthew. *Illuminations of Hildegard of Bingen*. Santa Fe: Bear & Co., 1985.

Giumelli, Claudio. "L'architettura dell'abbazia di Santa Scolastica." In *I monasteri benedettini di Subiaco*, edited by Claudio Giumelli, 11–66. Milano: Silvana Editoriale, 2002.

Gordley, Matthew E. *New Testament Christological Hymns: Exploring Texts, Contexts, and Significance*. Downers Grove, IL: IVP Academic, 2018.

Gräslund, Bo, and Neil Price. "Twilight of the Gods? The 'Dust Veil Event' of AD 536 in Critical Perspective." *Antiquity* 332 (2012): 428–43.

Hall, Roger L. *Simple Gifts: A Great American Folk Song*. Stoughton, MA: Pine Tree Productions, 2014.

Hamman, Adalbert Hamman. *Vie Liturgique et Vie Sociale*. Paris: Desclée & Cie, 1968.

Helms, Mary. "Sacred Landscape and the Early Medieval Cloister: Unity, Paradise, and the Cosmic Mountain." *Anthropos* 97 (2002): 435–53.

Hodges, Richard. *Light in the Dark Ages: The Rise and Fall of San Vincenzo al Volturno*. London and Ithaca: Duckworth Press/ Cornell University Press, 1997.

Hoffmann, Richard C. "Economic Development and Aquatic Ecosystems in Medieval Europe." *The American Historical Review* 101.3 (June 1996): 631–69.

Hoffmann, Richard C. *An Environmental History of Medieval Europe*. New York: Cambridge University Press, 2014.

Hughes, J. Donald. *Environmental Problems of the Greeks and Romans: Ecology in the Ancient Mediterranean*. Baltimore: Johns Hopkins University Press, 2014.

Jensen, Robin. *Baptismal Imagery in Early Christianity: Ritual, Visual, and Theological Dimensions*. Ada, MI: Baker Books, 2012.

Jensen, Robin. *Understanding Early Christian Art*. London: Routledge, 2000.

Kardong, Terrence. *The Life of St. Benedict by Gregory the Great: Translation and Commentary*. Collegeville, MN: Liturgical Press, 2009.

Klassen, John. "The Rule of Benedict and Environmental Stewardship." Public lecture, Sustainability Summit. College of Saint Benedict /Saint John's University, 2004. https://web.archive.org/web /20200809120950/https://www.csbsju.edu/sju-sustainability /about-us/benedictine-stewardship/values/klassen.

Klauser, Theodor. *A Short History of the Western Liturgy*. Translated by John Halliburton. London: Oxford University Press, 1969.

Krautheimer, Richard. *Rome: Profile of a City, 312–1308*. Princeton: Princeton University Press, 2000.

Lathrop, Gordon. *Holy Ground: A Liturgical Cosmology*. Minneapolis: Fortress Press, 2003.

LeClercq, Henri. "Graffites." In *Dictionnaire d'archéologie chrétienne et de liturgie*, edited by Fernand Cabrol and Henri LeClercq, 1453–542. Vol. 6.2. Paris: Libraire Letouzey et Ane, 1925.

LeVasseur, Todd, and Anna Peterson, eds. *Religion and Ecological Crisis: The "Lynn White Thesis" at Fifty*. New York: Routledge, 2017.

Llewellyn, Peter. *Rome in the Dark Ages*. New York: Praeger, 1971.

López, J. M. López, M. I. Pérez Millán, and A. B. González Avilés. "The Importance of Graphic Representation in Monastic Hydraulics." In *Water and Society III*, edited by C. A. Brebbia, 377–88. Southampton: Wessex Institute of Technology Press, 2015.

Mallarach, Josep-Maria. "Monastic Communities and Nature Conservation: Overview of Positive Trends and Best Practices in Europe and the Middle East." In *The Diversity of Sacred Lands in Europe*, edited by Josep-Maria Mallarach, Thymio Papayannis, and Rauno Väisänen. Gland, Switzerland: IUCN, 2012.

Mallarach, Josep-Maria, Josep Corcó, and Thymio Papayannis. "Christian Monastic Communities Living in Harmony with the Environment: An Overview of Positive Trends and Best Practices." *Studia Monastica* 56 (2014): 353–91.

Martimort, A. G. "Liturgical Signs." In *Principles of the Liturgy*, vol. 1 of *The Church at Prayer*, edited by A. G. Martimort and translated by Matthew O'Connell, 188–91. Collegeville, MN: Liturgical Press, 1987.

Martins, Ana M. T., and Jorge Carlos. "The Essence of Daylight in the Cistercian Monastic Church of S. Bento de Cástris, Évora, Portugal." *IOP Conference Series: Materials Science and Engineering* 245.5 (2017): 1–10.

Marucchi, Orazio. "Cross." In *The Catholic Encyclopedia*, edited by Charles Herbermann, 527. Vol. 4. New York: Robert Appleton, 1908.

Mathews, Thomas F. *The Clash of Gods: A Reinterpretation of Early Christian Art*. Princeton: Princeton University Press, 1993.

McAuliffe, Marie, and Anna Triandafyllidou, eds. *The World Migration Report 2022*. Geneva: United Nations International Organization for Migration, 2021.

McCormick, Michael, Ulf Büntgen, Mark A. Cane, Edward R. Cook, Kyle Harper, Peter Huybers, Thomas Litt, Stuart W. Manning, Paul Andrew Mayewski, Alexander F. M. More, Kurt Nicolussi, and Willy Tegel. "Climate Change during and after the Roman Empire: Reconstructing the Past from Scientific and Historical Evidence." *Journal of Interdisciplinary History* 43.2 (August 2012): 169–220.

McGann, Mary. *The Meal That Reconnects: Eucharistic Eating and the Global Food Crisis.* Collegeville, MN: Liturgical Press, 2020.

McGinn, Bernard. "St. Benedict as the Steward of Creation." *American Benedictine Review* 39.2 (1988): 161–76.

McNeil, John R. *The Mountains of the Mediterranean: An Environmental History.* Cambridge: Cambridge University Press, 1992.

Mensing, Scott A., Edward M. Schoolman, Irene Tunno, Paula J. Noble, Leonardo Sagnotti, Fabio Florindo, and Gianluca Piovesan. "Historical Ecology Reveals Landscape Transformation Coincident with Cultural Development in Central Italy since the Roman Period." *Scientific Reports* 8.2138 (2018); published online February 1, 2018, https://www.ncbi.nlm.nih.gov/pmc/articles/PMC5794987/.

Merton, Thomas. *Seasons of Celebration: Meditations on the Cycle of Liturgical Feasts.* Notre Dame, IN: Ave Maria Press, 1950.

Mitchell, Nathan. "The Liturgical Code in the Rule of Benedict." In *RB 1980: The Rule of St. Benedict in Latin and English with Notes*, edited by Timothy Fry, 379–408. Collegeville, MN: Liturgical Press, 1981.

Monachino, Vincenzo. *La Carità Cristiana a Roma.* Rome: Cappelli Editore, 1968.

Monastery of Christ in the Desert. "Sustainable Stewardship." *Monastery of Christ in the Desert*, 2022, accessed on November 15, 2022, https://christdesert.org/about/sustainable-stewardship/.

Murray, Peter and Linda. *The Oxford Dictionary of Christian Art.* Rev. ed. Oxford: Oxford University Press, 2013.

Nelson, Michael Paul, and Thomas J. Sauer. "The Long Reach of Lynn White Jr.'s 'The Historical Roots of Our Ecologic Crisis.'" *Ecology & Evolution* (December 13, 2016), accessed on September 30, 2022, https://ecoevocommunity.nature.com/posts/14041

-the-long-reach-of-lynn-white-jr-s-the-historical-roots-of-our
-ecologic-crisis.

Northcott, Michael S. *Place, Ecology and the Sacred: The Moral Geography of Sustainable Communities*. London: Bloomsbury, 2015.

Pantoni, Angelo. *L'Acropoli di Montecassino e Il Primitivo Monastero di San Benedetto*. Miscellanea Cassinese 43. Montecassino: Pubblicazioni Cassinesi, 1984.

Pastoral Constitution on the Church in the Modern World. In *Vatican Council II: The Conciliar and Postconciliar Documents*, edited by Austin Flannery. Collegeville, MN: Liturgical Press, 2014.

Permanent Delegation of Italy to the United Nations Educational, Scientific and Cultural Organization (UNESCO). "The Cultural Landscape of the Benedictine Settlements in Medieval Italy" (March 18, 2016), accessed on July 16, 2022, https://whc.unesco.org/en/tentativelists/6107/.

Pope Francis. *Laudato Si': On Care for Our Common Home*. Huntington, IN: Our Sunday Visitor, 2015.

Rech, Photina. *Wine and Bread*, translated by Heinz R. Kuehn. Chicago: Liturgy Training Publications, 1998.

Richards, Jeffrey. *The Popes and the Papacy in the Early Middle Ages, 476–752*. London: Routledge and Kegan Paul, 1979.

Rossing, Barbara. "Alas for the Earth! Lament and Resistance in Revelation 12." In *The Earth Story in the New Testament*, edited by Norman Habel and Vicky Balabanski, 180–92. London: Sheffield Academic Press, 2002.

Saroli, Michele, Michele Lancia, and Marco Petitta. "The Geology and Hydrogeology of the Cassino Plain (Central Apennines, Italy): Redefining the Regional Groundwater Balance." *Hydrogeology Journal* 27 (2019): 1563–79.

Seasoltz, R. Kevin. *A Sense of the Sacred: Theological Foundations of Christian Architecture and Art*. New York: Continuum, 2005.

Seshimo, Naoki. "Light and Proportion in Cistercian Monasteries." In *The Architectural League of New York* (July 17, 2002), accessed on July 25, 2021, https://archleague.org/article/light-and-proportion-in-the-cistercian-monasteries/.

Silecchia, Lucia. "*Laudato Si'* and the Tragedy of a 'Throwaway Culture.'" In *Catholic University of America Columbus School of Law*

Legal Studies, research paper no. 2017-2. Washington, DC: Catholic University of America, 2017.

Smith, Dennis. *From Symposium to Eucharist: The Banquet in the Early Christian World*. Minneapolis: Fortress Press, 2009.

Smith, Norman A. F. "The Roman Dams of Subiaco." *Technology and Culture* 11.1 (January 1970): 58–68.

Snyder, Graydon. *Ante Pacem: Archaeological Evidence of Church Life before Constantine*. Rev. ed. Macon, GA: Mercer University Press, 2003.

Snyder, Graydon. *Inculturation of the Jesus Tradition: The Impact of Jesus on Jewish and Roman Cultures*. Harrisburg, PA: Trinity Press International, 1999.

Squatriti, Paolo. *Water and Society in Early Medieval Italy, AD 400–1000*. Cambridge: Cambridge University Press, 2002.

Stark, Rodney. *The Rise of Christianity: How the Obscure, Marginal Jesus Movement Became the Dominant Religious Force in the Western World in a Few Centuries*. San Francisco: HarperSanFrancisco, 1997.

Steels, Paul. "Graffiti." In *The New Catholic Encyclopedia*, edited by William McDonald, 688–89. Vol. 3. New York: McGraw Hill, 1967.

Stroll, Mary. *The Medieval Abbey of Farfa: Target of Papal and Imperial Ambitions*. Leiden: Brill, 1997.

Sutera, Judith. "The Rule of Benedict." In *Green Monasticism: A Buddhist-Catholic Response to an Environmental Calamity*, edited by Donald Mitchell and William Skudlarek, 76–86. New York: Lantern Books, 2010.

Taylor, Bron, Gretel Van Wieren, and Bernard Daley Zaleha. "Lynn White Jr. and the Greening-of-Religion Hypothesis." *Conservation Biology* 30.5 (2016): 1000–1009.

Thurston, Bonnie Bowman. *Widows: A Women's Ministry in the Early Church*. Minneapolis: Fortress Press, 1989.

Tomei, Maria. "La villa di Nerone a Subiaco: scavi e ricerche." *Archeologia Laziale* 6 (1984): 250–59.

Torvend, Samuel. "The Banquet of God's Vulnerable Creation." In *Still Hungry at the Feast: Eucharistic Justice in the Midst of Affliction*, 50–65. Collegeville, MN: Liturgical Press, 2019.

Torvend, Samuel. "Welcoming Care of God's Creation in Liturgical Reform." In *In Spirit and Truth: A Vision of Episcopal Worship*, edited by Stephanie Budwey, Kevin Moroney, Sylvia Sweeney, and Samuel Torvend, 135–44. New York: Church Publishing, 2020.

Torvend, Samuel. "Welcoming the Earth to Christian Worship." *Call to Worship* 42.4 (2009): 1–7.

Trible, Phyllis. "Ecology and the Bible: The Dilemma of Dominion." *Canon & Culture* (January 2012): 5–16.

Turner, Victor. "Passages, Margins, and Poverty: Religious Symbols of Communitas." *Worship* 46.7 (August 1972): 390–412.

United States Conference of Catholic Bishops. "Renewing the Earth: An Invitation to Reflection and Action on the Environment in Light of Catholic Social Teaching." Washington, DC: USCC, 1992, accessed on December 15, 2022, https://www.usccb.org/resources/renewing-earth.

White, Lynn T., Jr. "The Historical Roots of Our Ecologic Crisis." *Science* 155.3767 (1967): 1203–7.

Wickham, Chris. *Early Medieval Italy: Central Power and Local Society 400–1000*. Ann Arbor: University of Michigan Press, 1989.

Wickham, Chris. "The *Terra* of San Vincenzo al Volturno in the 8th and 12th Centuries: The Historical Framework." In *San Vincenzo al Volturno: The Archaeology, Art, and Territory of an Early Medieval Monastery*, edited by Richard Hodges and John Mitchell, 227–58. Oxford: British Archaeological Reports, 1985.

Wybrew, Hugh. "Ceremonial." In *The Study of the Liturgy*, edited by Cheslyn Jones, Geoffrey Wainwright, and Edward Yarnold, 432–37. New York: Oxford University Press, 1978.

Index

Abbot, 98–100
Acasius of Constantinople, 47
Adalbert de Vogüé, 65–66
'adam, 66; 85; 129
   New Adam, 85; 114
Agapetus of Rome, 50–51
Alaric, 44
Ambrose, Autpert, 113
Ambrose of Milan, 79
Animals, 18–20; 21–25; 61–63;
    64–65; 127–130
   Human cooperation with, 65–66
   Lead the praise of God, 19–20
   Roman slaughter of, 18–19
Anio/Aniene River, 53–55
Anthony of Egypt, 62; 64; 128
Anthropocentrism, 86–88; 90; 133
Armed conflict
   As environmental weapon, 7–8
Augustine of Hippo, 24n62; 49

Basil of Caesarea, xii
Benedict of Nursia, xii; 45–46
   And absence of Christian
    education, 50–52
   And church leadership, 49–50
   And church privileges, 51
   And divestment of social
    privilege, 60; 73–74
   And food, 55–58
   And friendship with non-
    human creatures, 63–66

   And Roman church conflicts,
    47–48
   And stone, 69–72
   And water, 66–69
   As patron saint of ecology, 73
   As reformer, xiv
   As wild beast, 61–63
   Departure from Rome, 46; 52
   Fishing in the Anio River, 54–55
   In a cave, 58–60
   In nature, 72–74
   Living in an antistructure, 62
   With a raven, 63–66
Birds, 64; 127–128
Bishops' Committee on the
   Liturgy
   Environment and Art in Catholic
    Worship, 124n26
Black Plague, 103
Breuer, Marcel, 139

Capitalist materialism, 133
Carson, Rachel, 126–127
Chain of Being, 86–87; 128
Christian feasts and seasons
   Aligned with natural seasons,
    83–84
Church
   Imperialization, 38–44; 51–52
   Romanization, 42–43
   Wealth and privileges of clergy,
    48–50

Clement of Alexandria, 23n50;
    23n54; 24n63
Constantine, 39–41; 77
Constantinople, 40–41
Council of Nicaea, 40; 47
Creation
    Created and owned by God,
       87–89
    First gift of grace, 143
    Intrinsic value of, 88
    No romanticization of, 89–90
    Non-hierarchical, 86–87
    Not static but developing, 88–
       89; 115
    Objectification of, 112–113
    Sacred, 114–115
Crucifixion, 14–15; 28
Cunctos populos, 41–42

Daily Prayer; Liturgy of the
    Hours; Work of God:
    See Divine Office
Dawson, Ashley, 5
Deforestation, 5–7
Desertification, 5
Diocletian, 38–39
Divine Office, 75–112
    Autumnal and vernal
       equinoxes, 83–84
    Christ at the center, 77–79;
       81–82; 84–85; 119–122
    Prayer during the day, 75–80
    Prayer during the week, 80–82
    Praying with natural light,
       75–77; 136
    Praying with the seasons,
       82–86
    Psalms of creation, 86–94
Dubos, René, 73
Dust Veil Disaster, 103

Early Christian communities,
    marks of
    Aliens in an imperial culture,
       32–33
    Baptism, 30; 32
    Baptismal equality, 30
    Ethic of care for others, 33–35
    Eucharist, 30–31
    Healing practices, 31; 34–35
    House churches, 29–30
    Leadership, 31–32
    Martyrdom, 36–38
    Sacramental materiality, 23–25
    Structuralization, 32
Early Christian movement
    Imperialization, 38–44
    Revitalization movement, 35
    Social movement, 33
    Unpatriotic, 37
Early Christian worship, 22–27;
    30–31
    Ecophilic, 26
    Materiality of, 25–26
Early medieval agriculture, 101
Ecophilia, ecophilic, xiii; 26;
    94–96; 137
Edict of Milan, 39–40
Elijah, 58; 61; 64–65
Environmental justice
    And imperialism, 1
    And racism, 86–87

Fishing
    Benedict, 56–57
    Papal fishing rights, 105; 109
Francis, Pope
    *Laudato Si': On Care for Our
       Common Home*, ix; 112n27;
       129; 134
    Commodification of earth and
       its creatures, 134

Cruelty to animals condemned,
    129
Industrial waste, 134
Throwaway culture, 134; 137
Friendship with other creatures,
    127–130
Frontinus, 53n2; 57
Fuga mundi, 95; 100

Galerius, emperor, 39
Gladiators, 3
God
    Benevolent creator of light and
        darkness, 80
    Divine presence everywhere,
        66; 74; 81; 102
    Earth is God's home, 124–125
    Eternal Maker, 79–80
    Everlasting Rock, 71–72; 74
    Molder of the cosmos, 88
    Possessor of the creation, 91
    Provider for all creatures, 92–94
Gordley, Matthew, 12; 14
Gothic War, 103; 111; 115
Graffito blasfemo, 15
Gratian, 41
Gregory the Great, xii
    Care for Rome, 45–46
    Dialogues II, purpose of, 46–47;
        63; 72
Gyrovagues, 103–104

Hildegard of Bingen, 115
Hughes, Donald, 4
Humility, 63; 90; 130–132; 137
    And pride, 131
    Humus, 15; 70; 73
    Downward movement of, 90
Huskins, Olga, 126–127
Hymns
    Ambrosian, 79
    Colossian (1:15-20), 16–17

Johannine (1:1-18), 17–18; 113
Lucan (2:14), 9–10
Philippian (2:4-11), 13–14
Revelation (4:1–5:14), 18–21

Industrial Revolution
    And environmental degradation,
        87–88

Jerome, 64; 128
Jerusalem, environmental
    destruction of, 7–8
Jesus Christ
    A wisdom figure, 120–121
    Agent of creation, 74; 77–78; 120
    Displaces the emperor, 14; 15;
        17; 85–86
    Divestment from privilege,
        13–14
    Familiarity with earth and its
        creatures, 84–85; 121–122
    Firstborn of all creation, 82; 85;
        120–121
    Lamb of God, 19–22
    Nature images for, 22–25;
        137–138
    Servant, 13–14
    Sun of righteousness, 78
    Word of God, 17–18; 85
John the Baptist, 61–62
Justin Martyr, 31; 60

Kardong, Terence, xiii; 113–114;
    125n31
Kiel, Micah, 18
Kingdom of God, 2
    Alternative to the Kingdom of
        Caesar, 9–12
Klassen, John, xiii; 126n32; 132n39;
    135n46
Krautheimer, Richard, 42–43

Late Antique Little Ice Age, 57–58
Lawrence, Philip, xiii
Local ecology, 107–108; 125–127;
    141–142

Mary, Mother of God, 60; 83; 84n27
Mass of creation, 122–125
    Dependent on earth's gifts, 124
Merton, Thomas, 143
Michel, Virgil, xiv–xv
Mines, mining, 8n14
Monastery of Christ in the Desert,
    xi; 135–137
Monastery of Monte Cassino, x;
    84n27; 97; 100n14; 105; 106;
    108
Monastery of San Benedetto, 56
Monastery of San Clemente, 70
Monastery of San Vincenzo al
    Volturno, 105; 106; 108–109
Monastery of Santa Maria di
    Farfa, 105; 106; 109
Monastery of San Pietro al Monte,
    105
Monastery of Santa Scholastica, x;
    107
Monastic cellarer, 99–100; 113–114
Monastic conservation, 95–96;
    101–102; 104–105; 111–112;
    114; 136–137
Monastic diet, 56–57; 110
Monastic gardens, 101; 105–106;
    114
Monastic hydrology, 68–69
Monastic labor, 100–102
    Monastic laborers as the New
        Adam, 114
    Reversing Rome's environmen-
        tal degradation, 94–96
Monastic land, 115
    Praising God before human
        habitation, 136

Monastic spaces, 70–72; 98–99; 136
Monastic stones, 70–71
Mount Taleo, 56

New Jerusalem, 144

Odoacer, 44
Ovid, 3; 5
Ownership
    private, condemnation of, 91–92;
        109

Pandemics
    Early Christian response to, 34–35
Paul, the apostle, 29; 31–32; 99
Paul, the deacon, 108
Perpetua and Felicity, 37–38
Pilate, Pontius, 2
Pliny the Younger, 36–37
Pollution, 6–7; 8n14
Propertius of Assisi, 4
Psalms
    Creation, presence of, 86–94
    Psalm (9), 71
    Psalm (24), 91; 109
    Psalm (27), 71
    Psalm (29), 89
    Psalm (95), 88
    Psalm (96), 87
    Psalm (104), 87; 88; 93–94
    Psalm (142), 59
    Sung in one week, 86
    Resistance poetics, 9–22; 88

River of life, 55; 124–125; 144
Rivers
    Anio, 53–55; 66; 67
    Digentia, 54
    Farfa, 55
    Gari, 55
    Liri, 105
    Volturno, 55

Roman aqueducts, 54
Roman emperor, 2–4; 7; 9–10; 16
  As savior and lord of the earth,
    3–4; 10; 14; 91
Roman Empire, 1–3
  Colonizing power, 5–6
  Roman environmental
    degradation, 5–9
Romanus, 56
Rome
  Deforestation, 5
  Head of the world, 41; 43
  In decline, 41
  Pollution in, 6–7; 57
Rule of Benedict
  As a spiritual classic, 97–98
  Common sharing of all things,
    109–110
  Condemnation of private
    ownership, 91–92
  Conservation of land and
    water, 101–102
  Ecophilic spirit of, 115–116
  Frugality, 110–111
  Living in harmony with
    natural seasons, 82–84
  Materialism, 110
  Modesty, 107
  Primacy of love, 115
  Self-sufficiency, 107–111
  Sense of place, 98–100
  Stability, 99; 102–107; 137

Saint John's Abbey, xi; 139–141
Santa Pudenziana, church of
  Imperial image of Christ, 43–44

Simbruini Mountains, 54; 58; 68
Stark, Rodney, 35
Subiaco, xii; 53–74
Sutera, Judith, xiii; 99n13
Superfund sites, x; 130
Sustainable stewardship, 135–137

Tertullian of Carthage, 23n54; 31
Theodoric, 44; 47
Theodosius, xii; 41–42
Trajan, 18–19; 36
Tree of life, 125; 144
Turner, Victor, 62

United Nations Educational,
  Scientific, and Cultural
  Organization
  *The Cultural Landscape of the
  Benedictine Settlements in
  Medieval Italy*, ix–x; 95; 98;
  135
United States Conference of
  Catholic Bishops
  *Renewing the Earth: An Invita-
  tion to Reflection and Action on
  the Environment in Light of
  Catholic Social Teaching*, 142

Valentinian, 41
Vitruvius, 55

Walafrid of Strabo, 92
White, Lynn, 26; 117–118

Zeno, 47